SIMPSONS COMICS
SIMPSORAMA

Titan Books

To the loving memory of Snowball I:
9 lives never went so fast.

SIMPS-O-RAMA Copyright ©1995 & 1996 by
Bongo Entertainment, Inc. All rights reserved.

Published in the UK by Titan Books Ltd., 42-44 Dolben Street,
London SE1 OUP, under licence from Bongo Entertainment, Inc.

FIRST EDITION: AUGUST 1996
ISBN 1-85286-727-2
ISBN-13 9781852867270
13 15 17 19 20 18 16 14 12
Publisher: MATT GROENING
Managing Editor: JASON GRODE
Art Director / Editor: BILL MORRISON
Book Design: MARILYN FRANDSEN
Legal Guardian: SUSAN GRODE
Contributing Artists:
BILL MORRISON, TIM BAVINGTON, PHIL ORTIZ, LUIS ESCOBAR,
STEPHANIE GLADDEN, TIM HARKINS, NATHAN KANE, ERIC MOXCEY,
DAVID MOWRY, JEANNINE CROWELL, SCOTT SHAW!,
CHRIS UNGAR, SHAUN CASHMAN, CHRIS ROMAN
Contributing Writers:
BILL MORRISON, GARY GLASBERG, ROB HAMMERSLEY,
TODD J. GREENWALD, SCOTT M. GIMPLE, BARRY DUTTER,
JON AIBEL, GLENN BERGER, JEFF ROSENTHAL, SCOTT SHAW!

PRINTED IN ITALY

CONTENTS

A WARNING...

The contents of this book are under pressure. This is your first warning. Keep tightly closed in a cool, dry place. Do not point at face. Shake well before using. Batteries not included. Do not shake this book excessively. May cause drowsiness. All sales final. Intentional misuse of this book will render warranty void. Contents may have settled during shipping. Do not read this book by an open flame. This is your second warning. For external use only. Keep hands inside vehicle at all times. Harmful if swallowed. Watch for falling rocks. Rinse and repeat. Do not back up over this book—severe tire damage may result. Apply ointment sparingly. Do not remove this page under penalty of law. Report all suspicious activity to authorities immediately. Do not puncture or throw this book in fire. All shoplifters will be prosecuted. This is your final warning. Keep out of reach of impressionable adults. Complaints? Dial 1-555-EAT-MY-SHORTS. You have been warned.

MATT GROENING
Bongo Comics Group

NED FLANDERS TOP FORTY

"THESE ARE A FEW OF MY FAVORITE THINGS"

1. Family togetherness nights.

2. My "better half"..."the ol' ball 'n' chain. (Hee hee, just kiddin', Maude!)

3. Yellow ribbons on oak trees.

4. My new Lawn Begone MX-7 GrassMaster tractor-mower.

5. **Bob Hope specials.**

6. Pants with just a skosh more room in the seat and thighs.

7. The impassioned rhetoric of Reverend Lovejoy.

8. Halogen lighting.

9. Stick-to-itiveness.

10. My new AudioCratic 48-disc CD player with fully uncontrollable no-access random play.

11. Yellow ribbons on flagpoles.

12. **Natural law.**

13. Waiters who introduce themselves.

14. The Ice Capades.

15. The heady mixture of politics and religion.

16. **Florence Henderson.**

17. Cordless power tools.

18. Traditional American Family Values.

19. Feelin' groovy.

20. Those new, super-tasty low-sodium snack foods.

21. Talking with "The Man Upstairs."

22. **My new 64-inch drive-in screen TV.**

23. Yellow ribbons on car antennas.

24. Theme restaurants.

25. The power of positive thinking.

26. **That cozy way my jogging suit feels when it's fresh out of the dryer.**

27. Quality time with Todd and Rod.

28. My new HeartAttacker-2000 deluxe Step-Meister exerciser.

29. Dinner theatre.

30. The simple satisfaction of a job well done.

31. The jazzy song stylings of La Streisand.

32. **Made-for-TV movies.**

33. Maude's meatloaf.

34. Good ol' American know-how.

35. War movies with dance music soundtracks.

36. *Reader's Digest*'s "Life in These United States."

37. **My new WeedBeater cordless Weasel-Wacker.**

38. Letting my inner-child out to play.

39. Yellow ribbons on high-voltage utility poles.

40. **Spunk.**

PLEASE, NED! SUCH *LANGUAGE*, IN FRONT OF *THE CHILDREN!* NOW WHAT DID I DO THAT WAS SO *TERRIBLE?*

OH, COME ON, MOTHER! YOU KNOW *DARNED* WELL THAT YOU CAN'T MAKE *S'MORES* WITHOUT DEEELICIOUS *CHOCOLATE*, AND *YOU* FORGOT TO *BRING* IT!

GRAMMIES

MARSH MELLOWS

WELL, JUST SANDWICH THE *MARSHMALLOWS* BETWEEN THE *GRAHAM CRACKERS* AND CALL IT SOMETHING *ELSE!*

BLASPHEMY!!

A FLANDERS CAMPEROONIE WITHOUT S'MORES IS LIKE...LIKE CHRISTMAS WITHOUT *FIGGY PUDDING!*

≶SIGH≷ NED, WHERE ARE YOU GOING?!

I NEED TO BLOW OFF SOME STEAM. I'M GOING TO FIND MYSELF A NICE PIECE OF *KNOTTY PINE* AND DO SOME HARDCORE *WHITTLING!!*

AUGUST 31, 2:47 PM.

NOW NOW, MAUDE. THREE WEEKS ISN'T *THAT* LONG FOR NED TO BE MISSING. REMEMBER, THE LORD WORKS IN HIS OWN *TIME*!

HE'S RIGHT. AN EXPERIENCED JUNIOR CAMPER LEADER COULD LIVE FOR *WEEKS* IN THESE WOODS. THERE'S A WHOLE FOREST FULL OF NUTS AND BERRIES OUT THERE, AND MOST OF THEM AREN'T ALL *THAT* POISONOUS!

:SOB! SNIFF!: I HAVEN'T GIVEN UP HOPE. IT'S JUST THAT WE HAD AN A-R-G-U-M-E-N-T THAT NIGHT AND I FEEL LIKE IT'S ALL *MY* FAULT!

DON'T BLAME *YOURSELF,* MA'AM. WE *ALL* HAVE OUR FAMILY SQUABBLES. AND NED DID THE RIGHT THING BY TAKING TIME OUT TO *COOL OFF.* THINGS COULD HAVE GOTTEN VERY UGLY.

HI, DADDY! CAN I GO FOR A SWIM WHILE THEY LOOK FOR THE *DEAD GUY?*

:GASP:

WHY YOU LITTLE...

HEH, HEH! DON'T BE ALARMED. JUST A BIT OF *FIRM* PARENTING. I SAW A FATHER DO THIS TO HIS SON ON TV.

SIR, WE *FOUND* SOMETHING IN THE *HIGH GRASS!*

WHAT *IS* IT, RANGER?!

HEAVENS TO *BETSY*...

CLUNK!

IT'S A GIANT *COCKTAIL TOOTHPICK!*

IT'S A SIGN FROM *GOD!*

IT'S ONE OF NED'S *WHITTLE STICKS!*

ARTS AND CRAFTS MEANT *EVERYTHING* TO HIM. HE'D *NEVER* ABANDON HIS *STICK!*

OKEY DOKEY

WELL, THAT'S *THAT!* NOW GET ME OUTTA THIS GOD FORSAKEN *HELL HOLE*, BEFORE IT GETS DARK AND THE *SQUIRREL-RAVAGED CARCASS OF NED FLANDERS* RISES FROM THE DEAD AND COMES AFTER US SEEKING *REVENGE*...

FWAP!

UH, HEH, HEH! I MEAN, UH, WHO'S UP FOR A BITE TO EAT?

I BELIEVE A *CONCILIATORY PRAYER* IS IN ORDER. BUT FIRST, I MUST *ANNOINT* MYSELF WITH *OIL!*

EASY BAKE SPF-2

OH MIGHTY *RA*...ER, I MEAN, DEAR HEAVENLY FATHER--

NED, MY DARLING, WHERE *ARE* YOU?!

DON'T BE SO *SURE*, MOM! HE COULD BE A *FLESH-EATING ZOMBIE!*

D'OH! I KNEW IT WAS TOO GOOD TO BE *TRUE!*

DOES THIS MEAN I DON'T GET TO KEEP HIS *MOTOR HOME?*

HOMER, HIS *FAMILY* STILL OWNS *THAT!*

WAP!

GEE WILLIKERS, MI FAMILIA! IF I KNEW I'D GET *THIS* KIND OF WELCOME, I'D HAVE GOTTEN LOST IN THE WOODS *BEFORE!*

OH, *DADDY!* WE MISSED YOU *SO MUCH!*

GOLLY, LISTEN TO MY RUMBLEDY-RUMBLER! I'M SO HUNGRY I COULD EAT A WHOLE BOX OF COMMUNION WAFERS!

GRRRRRRRRG!

JUUUST KIDDING!!!

WHAT'S *WRONG,* SIS?

BART, DO YOU NOTICE ANYTHING *DIFFERENT* ABOUT *NED FLANDERS?*

YEAH! *P.U.!* THE GUY *STINKS!*

EXACTLY! REMEMBER WHEN THE CHURCH HAD THAT FUNDRAISER, *"GET GRITTY FOR GOD?"* HE WENT FOR *FORTY DAYS AND FORTY NIGHTS* WITHOUT TAKING A BATH, AND STILL SMELLED *DAISY FRESH!*

HMMMM, I WONDER...

DEAR DIARY, TODAY I WILL STRAY FROM TELLING YOU MY INNERMOST THOUGHTS AND FEELINGS BECAUSE I BELIEVE BART AND I HAVE UNCOVERED SOMETHING TRULY MYSTERIOUS, AND I JUST *HAVE* TO TELL YOU ABOUT IT.

EVER SINCE NED FLANDERS'S RETURN TO CIVILIZATION, WE'VE NOTICED A STRIKING *CHANGE* IN HIS PERSONALITY.

URRP!

MOST OF THE NEIGHBORS ARE BLAMING HIS BEHAVIOR ON *POST TRAUMATIC STRESS SYNDROME.* HOWEVER, BART AND I AREN'T CONVINCED.

I'M WITH STUPID

I SUPPOSE WANDERING AIMLESSLY THROUGH THE WOODS FOR WEEKS WITHOUT HUMAN CONTACT WOULD CAUSE EVEN THE MOST *DEVOUT* MAN TO GO A *LITTLE* INSANE...

GIVE ME THAT ICE CREAM CONE, LITTLE YOUNGSTER!

WOOHOO! WAY TO GO, FLANDERS!

HE'S TAKEN THE TIME-HONORED TRADITION OF STEALING CANDY FROM A BABY AND GIVEN IT A BRAND NEW TWIST!

YOINK!

WAPPETTA-
WAPPETTA-
WAPPETTA!

...BUT NED FLANDERS ALWAYS SEEMED *DIFFERENT!*

HIS FAITH ALWAYS SEEMED TO GIVE HIM THE POWER TO OVERCOME SUCH EMOTIONAL OBSTACLES.

HEY, KIDDLEY-DEES! ENJOY YOUR FREE TIME WHILE YOU *CAN!* DON'T LET THE FACT THAT *SCHOOL* STARTS *TOMORROW* RUIN YOUR LAST DAY OF *FREEDOM!*

IT WAS OBVIOUS THAT *SOMEONE* OR *SOMETHING* WAS AFFECTING HIM. SURE, IT MAY HAVE BEEN OVEREXPOSURE TO SOME ULTRA-CONSERVATIVE *RADIO PERSONALITY,* OR POSSIBLY LACK OF *FIBER* IN HIS *DIET.* BUT I'M WILLING TO BET IT WAS DUE TO SOME KIND OF *UNEXPLAINED PHENOMENON.*

FOR A GOOD TIME, CALL MAUDE

EVEN *I* WOULDN'T GO *THAT* FAR!

YET!

WHAT WILL FLANDERS DO *NEXT?*

SEPT. 14, 3:40 PM - *THE TOKYO NATIONAL BANK OF SPRINGFIELD.*

BRRIING!

STOP HIM! HELP! WE'VE BEEN ROBBED!

OKILLY-DOKILLY, EVERYBODY! THIS IS A *STICK-UP.* START SINGING *LIL' RABBIT FOO FOO,* AND NO ONE WILL GET *HURT!*

AND I WANT THE *LONG* VERSION!

SAY YOUR PRAYERS, SMILEY!

BANG!

BANG! BANG!

SPLORTCH!

OW! THANKS FOR THINKIN' ABOUT MY AFTER-LIFE, OLD TIMER!

OOOF!

THWAK!

SORRY, BART! NO TIME TO CHAT! I'M IN THE MIDDLE OF A TEENSY FEDERAL OFFENSE! SAY HELLO TO YOUR FOLKS, WILL YA? TOODLES!

BANG! BANG!

V.RROOOM!

SWEET MOTHER MCCREE! HE'S LEAVING A TRAIL OF GREEN GOOP! WE WERE RIGHT! FLANDERS MAY NOT BE HUMAN AFTER ALL!

HMMM...THIS IS GETTING SERIOUS. I WONDER WHAT MCBAIN WOULD DO IN A SITUATION LIKE THIS?

McBAIN BITES

US STOP

SEPT. 15, 7:15 AM – THE ESTATE OF RAINIER WOLFCASTLE A.K.A. McBAIN.

GOOD MORNING, SIR. HOW WAS YOUR SWIM TODAY?

A THOUSAND PARDONS, MR. WOLFCASTLE.

HOW MANY TIMES DO I HAFF TO TELL YOU, FILL DAH POOL WIT GLACIER WATAH! CHLORINE MAKES ME TINGLE!

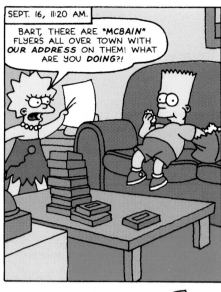

SEPT. 16, 11:20 AM.

BART, THERE ARE "MCBAIN" FLYERS ALL OVER TOWN WITH *OUR ADDRESS* ON THEM! WHAT ARE YOU *DOING*?!

WELCOME TO THE FIRST ANNUAL BART SIMPSON *MCBAIN-ATHON!* TWENTY-FOUR HOURS OF GUT-BURSTING, HEAD-CRUNCHING, BULLET-RIDDEN ACTION, VOID OF ANY STORYLINE AND *JAM-PACKED* WITH LAME-BUT-MEMORABLE ONE-LINERS. I FIGURED SINCE I RENTED SO MANY TAPES, I'D TRY TO RECOUP MY EXPENSES.

AND IF I DON'T *PAY?!*

KA-BASH!

OOPS!

RT WING

YOWZAH! DOES THAT ANSWER YOUR QUESTION?

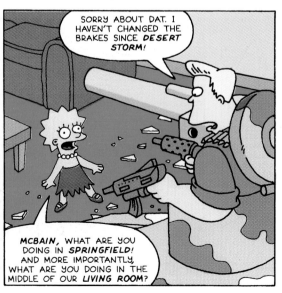

SORRY ABOUT DAT. I HAVEN'T CHANGED THE BRAKES SINCE *DESERT STORM!*

MCBAIN, WHAT ARE YOU DOING IN *SPRINGFIELD!* AND MORE IMPORTANTLY, WHAT ARE YOU DOING IN THE MIDDLE OF OUR *LIVING ROOM?*

PLEASE, CALL ME *RAINIER!* I CAME TO INVESTIGATE DA WIMPY *BANK ROBBER* WIT DA *GREEN BLOOD!*

THEN I SAW DA MCBAIN SIGNS WIT DA ARROWS, AND FOLLOWED DEM *HERE!*

SEPT. 16, 12:05 PM - *KRUSTYBURGER STORE #37.*

{SIGH}... I CAN'T BELIEVE MY MODEL OF MALE MACHISMO IS EATING A *VEGETARIAN KRUSTY MIDWAY MEAL!*

IT'S DA ONLY WAY TO GET DA FREE TOY!

SO ANYWAY, THIS IS A *SAMPLE* OF THE *GREEN GOO* THAT TRICKLED OUT OF *NED FLANDERS'S BODY!*

MMM... LOOKS LIKE *GUACAMOLE!*

AFTER A THOROUGH MICROSCOPIC ANALYSIS, WE DETERMINED THAT THE FLUID IS COMPOSED OF CHEMICALS OF AN *UNEARTHLY NATURE!*

GOOD! I LIKE *NATURE!*

HUMOR HIM.

PSST! DON'T TURN AROUND! I'M HERE TO LIGHTEN YOUR LOAD!

{GULP} ARE YOU FROM THE *IRS?* I SWEAR, DA SKI TRIP TO GSTAAD WAS *WORK-RELATED!*

GO WHERE FLANDERS *DISAPPEARED,* AND LOOK FOR SOMETHING *VERY WEIRD!*

AAH, *CRYPTIC MESSAGES!* BUT WE DON'T EVEN KNOW WHERE THE CAMPSITE *IS!*

I'LL ASK FOR *DIRECTIONS!*

RRRIIIP

WHERE *IS* HE?!

:GULP: UM, WOULD YOU LIKE THAT *TO GO*, SIR?

LOOK, GUYS! HE LEFT US A *CLUE!*

OF *COURSE!* THE FLANDERS FAMILY NEVER TRAVELS *ANYWHERE* WITHOUT A CUSTOM-MADE AUTO CLUB *TRIP-TIK!* THIS SHOULD LEAD US STRAIGHT TO THE *CAMPSITE!!*

SEPT. 16, 3:45 PM – *SPRINGFIELD NATIONAL PARK.*

WHEW! I'M *BEAT*, MAN!

I HAD NO IDEA THE MOUNTAINS COULD BE THIS *HOT!*

DON'T BE SUCH *PANSIES!* IN *AUSTRIA* I USED TO CLIMB THE ALPS JUST TO GET TO *KINDERGARTEN!*

GIMME A BREAK, *MCBLOWHARD!* IF THIS WAS A *MCBAIN* FLICK, YOU'D JUST JUMP OUT OF A HELICOPTER AND LAND RIGHT IN THE MIDDLE OF THE *CAMPSITE!*

YAH, TOO BAD MY *STUNT DOUBLE* IS BUSY HAVING HIS SPINE RELOCATED.

IF MY CALCULATIONS ARE CORRECT, NED FLANDERS DISAPPEARED IN *THIS IMMEDIATE AREA*. OUR MYSTERY TIPSTER SAID TO LOOK FOR SOMETHING *WEIRD*, BUT *I* DON'T SEE ANYTHING *UNUSUAL!*

GOTTA...*REST!* CAN'T...GO...ANY ...*FURTHER!*

WUMP!

UH-OH, WHAT'S WRONG WIT THE LITTLE *PACK BOY?*

ASIDE FROM BEING *DEHYDRATED*, I BELIEVE MY BROTHER HAS DRAWN OUR ATTENTION TO AN *IMPORTANT CLUE!*

WE SEEM TO BE IN SOME KIND OF STRANGE *MATTED GRASSY AREA!*

BIG *DEAL!* I GOT A WHOLE *YAHD* LIKE DIS FROM MY *POOCH* DOING HIS *BUSINESS!*

I SAY WE SEND *MR. TOUGH GUY* UP A TREE FOR A *BETTER LOOK!* OR IS HE AFRAID HE MIGHT GET HIS *NAILS* DIRTY?!

HOW'D YOU LIKE A CLOSER LOOK AT MY NAILS WHEN I WRAP MY *FINGERS* AROUND YOUR PUNY LITTLE *THROAT?!*

⦃GULP⦄ I SUDDENLY HAVE A STRANGE *URGE* TO HUG SOME *BARK!*

SOON...

WELL BART, WHAT DO YOU *SEE*?!

RAINIER HAS A *BALD SPOT*!

I SHAVED IT FOR A ROLE THEY OFFERED *CONNERY*!

¡GASP¡ UH-OH! I *THINK* WE'RE IN TROUBLE!

WHAT *IS* IT, BART?!

DO YOU SEE *MARIA*?

SIDESHOW BOB!!

YOU WERE EXPECTING *E.T.*? GOOD OF YOU TO COME, BART. I AM SO LOOKING *FORWARD* TO DISINTEGRATING YOUR PUNY LITTLE BODY, *BONE* BY *BONE*!

WHO ARE YOUR *FRIENDS*, BOB?

OH, FORGIVE ME FOR BEING SO *RUDE*. MAY I INTRODUCE *KANG* AND *KODOS*-- TWO ALIENS WITH MORE FREQUENT FLYER MILES THAN ANYONE ON *RIGEL-4*!

HA! FLYER MILES! HA-HA!

KANG, IF ONLY ONE OF OUR *BRETHREN* HAD HAD THE JOCULAR ABILITY OF *BROTHER SIDESHOW*, WE'D BE LAUGHING FOR *ALL MILLENIUM*!!

YAH, HE'S A REGULAR *JERRY LEWIS*!

I THOUGHT YOU WERE IN *JAIL*, BOB.

I *WAS*! QUITE COMFORTABLE, TOO, UNTIL THAT BUFFOON *CANKER* HELPED ME ESCAPE.* FORTUNATELY, I WAS LUCKY ENOUGH TO BE *ABDUCTED* BY MY CHARMING ONE-EYED *HOSTS*!

CHECK OUT BARTMAN #4.

AT THE TIME, THEY WERE KIDNAPPING *HUMAN SPECIMENS* AND CREATING EVIL CLONE-LIKE *DUPLICATES* TO DEPOSIT BACK ON EARTH. THEY WANTED TO MAKE *ME* THEIR *NEXT* SUBJECT, HOWEVER, FINDING IT IMPOSSIBLE TO IMPROVE ON *PERFECTION*, I TOLD THEM...

♪ I'VE GOTTA BE *MEEE*!!! ♪

HOORAY! BRAVO!

ALL OF RIGEL-4 REVERE THE COCKNEY SONG STYLINGS OF *ANTHONY NEWLEY*!

AFTER I WOWED THEM WITH MY ONE-MAN PERFORMANCE OF *"STOP THE WORLD I WANT TO GET OFF"*, THEIR EVIL CLONE TECHNOLOGY WAS AT *MY* DISPOSAL!

LOCATING *NED FLANDERS*, I IMMEDIATELY ABDUCTED HIM FROM HIS CAMPSITE, IN HOPES THAT AN *EVIL FLANDERS CLONE* COULD BE PROGRAMMED TO MURDER A CERTAIN *ANNOYING LITTLE NEIGHBOR*. I WOULD HAVE MY REVENGE ON YOU, BART, AND, OF COURSE, NONE OF THIS COULD BE TRACED BACK TO *MOI!*

A PITY, THE CLONE *DISAPPEARED* BEFORE BRINGING MY PLAN TO *FRUITION!*

A MEANINGLESS GAME WE PLAY WHEN WE'RE BORED. SORT OF A RIGELLIAN VERSION OF *TIC-TAC-TOE!*

AND WHAT ABOUT THE *CROP CIRCLES?*

THE *RED BUTTON* ON THE CONSOLE CONTROLS *EVERYTHING!* WHEN WE DISCOVERED YOUR LITTLE SEARCH PARTY, I CREATED THE *"NO BART"* GRAPHIQUE IN AN EFFORT TO DRAW YOU INTO AN ABDUCTABLE LOCATION.

NOW IT APPEARS I'M GOING TO HAVE TO ELIMINATE YOU *MYSELF!* HOW DO YOU FEEL ABOUT *PRE-DEATH EMBALMING,* BART?!

EEEP!

DON'T *WORRY,* BART. I'VE GOT AN *IDEA!*

WRROOOOOO

ACH! WHAT IN TH' NAME O' *NESSIE...?* SOUNDS LIKE THE *WAILIN'* OF A *BANSHEE!*

DAG BLAST YE NO GOOD *SPACE BLAGGARDS!* I'LL TEACH YE WHAT A *SCOTSMAN* KIN *DYOOO!!*

SCOTSMEN FIGHT LIKE WEE LASSIES

KIDS TODAY GET TOO MUCH VIOLENCE FROM TV AND MOVIES. BACK IN MY DAY IT WAS *RIGHT OUTSIDE* YOUR *WINDOW,* AND YOU COULD EXPERIENCE IT ON A NICE SUMMER DAY. BUT THAT WAS A TIME WHEN JUSTICE RODE A HORSE NAMED *VIOLENCE*. NO, I DON'T THINK JUSTICE HAD A HORSE BACK THEN, HE COULDN'T *AFFORD* IT. EVEN THOUGH LIFE WAS CHEAPER; YOU COULD GET A SARSAPARILLA FOR *A PENNY* AT THE OLD DRY GOODS STORE. IT REMINDS ME OF A STORY...

THE KWIK-E AND THE DEAD!

IN 1897, *TROUBLE* CAME TO SPRINGFIELD. *JEBEDIAH* COULDN'T HAVE KNOWN THAT THE TOWN HE FOUNDED RESTED ON A *GIANT OIL FIELD*. WILDCAT INDUSTRIALIST, *MONTGOMERY BURNS,* STAKED A CLAIM TO THE OIL DEPOSIT, AND THE IRON HORSE, GUNFIGHTERS, AND SOME FELLA SELLING FISH 'N' CHIPS FOLLOWED HIM INTO TOWN...

MOE'S SALOON

HORSE SPURS-N-SUCH 'R' US

WESTERN STUFF BANK

I TELL YA', THERE'S SOMETHIN' *ODD* 'BOUT THAT INDIAN.

WELL, AT LEAST HE AIN'T *TROUBLE* LIKE BURNS AND HIS RUFFIANS.

LIKE MOST TOWNS OF THE TIME, THE MAIN SOCIAL ATTRACTION WAS THE LOCAL SALOON. THAT ALL CHANGED WHEN OLD MAN DEEVERS ACCIDENTALLY DISCOVERED THAT YOU COULD SLIDE DOWN MT. SPRINGFIELD ON A POTATO SACK WITHOUT TEARING UP YOUR BACKSIDE. BUT, AT THE TIME, THE SALOON WAS THE PLACE TO HAVE A DRINK AND MEET A NICE GAL...

NOW, MARGIE, I WANT YOU TO WORK THE MEN BETTER.

WHAT KIND OF GUY WANTS TO COME TO A SALOON WHERE THE LADIES AREN'T...*FRIENDLY*?

MMM, *BEER*.

HI, THERE, STRANGER, WHAT'S YOUR *PLEASURE*?

NOT INTERESTED. *BEEER!*

HEY, SHERIFF, I HEARD OLD MONTY'S GONNA PUT A *HOLE* STRAIGHT THRU THAT *BADGE* THERE FOR LETTIN' THE KWIK-E FELLA SET UP A SHOP HERE IN TOWN.

SPEW!!

WELL, AH, HEY, THERE, MISTER, INTERESTED IN A *CARD* GAME?

I JUST WANTED A *DRINK*.

IF YOU PLAY, I'LL FIX YOU UP WITH A BEER *AND* MARGERIE.

YEAH, YEAH, AND MARGERIE, TOO.

I LIKE THE SOUND OF THAT...*BEER*.

NO ONE IS REALLY SURE WHAT HAPPENED NEXT, AND I DON'T EVEN REMEMBER IF I WAS *ACTUALLY THERE*. IN FACT, I MAY NOT HAVE EVEN BEEN *ALIVE* YET. BUT, THE CITIZENS OF SPRINGFIELD FOUND COURAGE FROM THE SACRIFICE OF THE NEW SHERIFF, EVEN THOUGH HE WAS *DEAD*. I THINIK THEY WERE OFF THEIR NUTS. THEY SHOULD HAVE LET BURNS TAKE OVER THE TOWN. I BET THERE WOULDN'T BE SO MANY STRIP MALLS NOW IF EVERYONE HAD CAVED INTO BURNS BACK THEN. BUT *NOOO*, THEY HAD TO REBEL...

YOU SHOT THE SHERIFF, BUT YOU DIDN'T SHOOT HIS NEW *DEPUTY*!

OR ME!

OR ME!

OR ME!

LET'S *GET* 'EM!

RUN, SMITTY, IT'S A PROLETARIAT UPRISING!

HEAR ME, SPRINGFIELD, YOU HAVE NOT HEARD THE *LAST* OF MONTGOMERY BURNS!...

...I'LL *OWN* THIS TOWN! MAYBE NOT TODAY, BUT SOMEDAY YOU'LL ALL BE WORKING FOR *MEEEE*!

THE BULLET HIT THE *PIE TIN*!

MMM, CHERRY.

GOOD FRIEND NEW SHERIFF, YOU ARE *ALIVE*.

OH, I DON'T KNOW WHAT I'M TALKING ABOUT ANYMORE. STUPID TV FILLS YOUR MIND WITH *MARBLES*. THAT REMINDS ME OF WHEN THEY BROUGHT THE *OLYMPICS* TO SPRINGFIELD BACK IN '23, OR WAS THAT '32?... HMMM, COULD'VE BEEN TIDDLY-WINKS ...I GUESS.

THE END

STORY — W.E. HOLLIDAY
PENCILS — LUIS ESCOBAR
INKS — TIM HARKINS & TIM BAVINGTON
LETTERING — MIKE SAKAMOTO
COLOR — NATHAN KANE
MAN WITH NO NAME — MATT GROENING

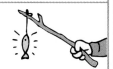

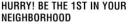

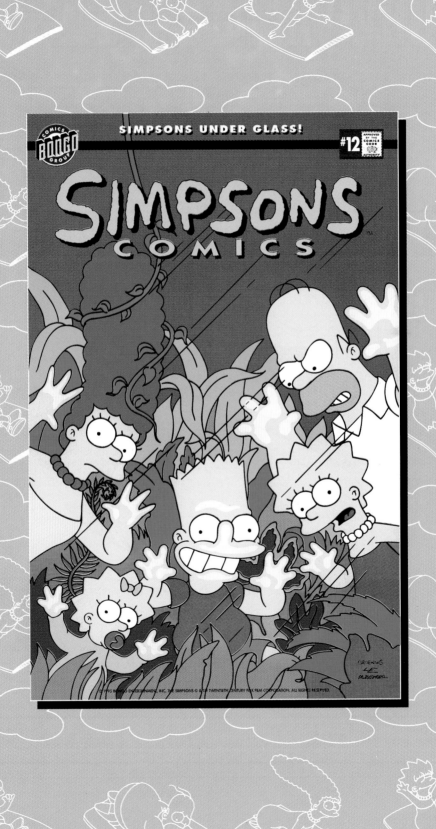

SURVIVAL of the FATTEST!

DESTRUCTION! BLOOD! WAR! TERROR HAS STRUCK EVERYWHERE!!

BAM!

SCRIPT	PENCILS	INKS	LETTERING	COLOR	CLIMATE CONTROLLER
ROB HAMMERSLEY & TODD J. GREENWALD	ERIC MOXCEY	TIM BAVINGTON	MIKE SAKAMOTO	ELECTRIC CRAYON	MATT GROENING

...SPRINGFIELD.

WHAT ARE YOUR THOUGHTS ON THE BIOSPHERE COMING TO SPRINGFIELD?

HI, MOM! I'M ON TV! UURRP!

...ENOUGH ABOUT MY BITTER DIVORCE. NOW THE NEWS... AFTER A LONG AND EXHAUSTIVE SELECTION PROCESS, SPRINGFIELD HAS BEEN CHOSEN AS THE SITE OF THE NEXT ENVIRONMENTAL RESEARCH BIOSPHERE. WE GO TO THE SCENE JUST MINUTES AGO.

A BIMBO-SPHERE! WOO-HOO! IT'S ABOUT TIME THIS TOWN GOT ANOTHER STRIP JOINT!

NO, DAD, IT'S A BIOSHPERE -- A SCIENCE EXPERIMENT.

HUH?

A SELF-CONTAINED ANIMATED ENVIRONMENT.

HUH?

IT'S SORT OF LIKE A HUMAN HABITRAIL.

OH, I GET IT.

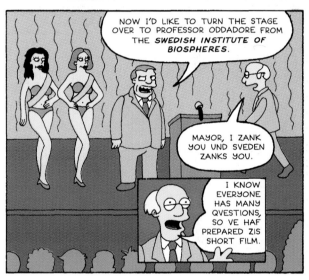

43

OUR FIRST TEST IS DESIGNED TO SEE HOW YOU WOULD SURVIVE IN THE WILD USING YOUR *SLINGSHOTS*. THE OBJECT IS TO ATTACK THE HUNTERS...

SHOOP!

...AND PROTECT THE HUNTED.

SPROING!

GOTCHA, DOC. LET'S GO KICK SOME *JUNGLE BUTT!*

DOINK!

SORRY. I THOUGHT I SAW SOMETHING.

THUNK!

THOK

NICE SHOT, DAD.

WHY YOU LITTLE...

HOLD ON A MINUTE, FOLKS! YOU'RE SUPPOSED TO ATTACK THE *ANIMALS*, NOT *EACH OTHER!*

KRAK!

OW!

THAT IS ALL WE'LL BE NEEDING FROM YOU TODAY. TAKE YOUR SCORECARD TO THE REGISTRATION DESK.

BUT WHAT ABOUT THE OTHER TESTS?

I'VE SEEN JUST ABOUT *ALL* I NEEDED TO SEE.

THE RESULTS WILL BE ANNOUNCED ON TV *TONIGHT*.

Chances of Survival 0%

HOW'D WE DO, DAD?

Chances of Survival 100%

WE DID *GREAT*! YOU SHOULD BE *PROUD* TO BE A SIMPSON.

THAT NIGHT...

VE ARE PROUD TO ANNOUNCE DAT THERE VERE *TWO* FAMILIES DAT SCORED PERFECTLY ON OUR EXAMS. SO, VE SELECTED ZEM *BOTH*. FIRST, ZE *HOMER SIMPSON FAMILY*.

BIOSPHERE

PRESS CONFERENCE

YES! WE'RE *NUMBER ONE*!

UND ZE *NED FLANDERS* FAMILY.

AAAAAAAAAAHHHHHH!!!

SEVERAL DAYS LATER...

I HEREBY ANNOUNCE THE OFFICIAL **OPENING** AND, ER, CLOSING OF THE SPRINGFIELD BIOSPHERE!

POP!

PSSSSSSSST!

AFTER A SPEEDY RECONSTRUCTION...

ENOUGH WITH THE CEREMONIAL MUMBO-JUMBO. GET YOUR **GUINEA PIG BUTTS** IN THERE.

KLUNK

LAST ONE TO BUILD THEIR HUT IS A ROTTEN **OINKELY-DOINKELY**.

BUILD? I THOUGHT THEY SAID ALL WE HAD TO DO IS PICK THE HUT WE WANTED.

YES-ER-OONY. YOU PICK THE HUT YOU WANT TO BUILD. IT'S ALL IN THIS HANDY-DANDY **SURVIVAL GUIDE** THEY GAVE US. WHERE'S YOURS?

BIO-GUIDE THE DIFFERENCE BETWEEN LIFE AND DEATH

UH, I DIDN'T GET ONE.

WELL, IF YOU NEED ANY HELP MY USUAL NEIGHBORLY **HELPING HAND** IS GOOD RIGHT HERE IN THE BIOSPHERE.

LET'S GET ONE THING STRAIGHT HERE, FLANDERS. I CAN TAKE CARE OF **MY FAMILY** JUST FINE. THE LAST THING I NEED IS HELP FROM **YOU!**

YOUR BARN DOOR'S OPEN.

THANKS.

ZZIP!

LATER...

FINISHED! WELL, WHAT DO YOU KNOW, I'M **DONE** AND MR. HELPING HAND HASN'T EVEN **STARTED**.

SLICE!

SPA-DOING!

WOW, **SWEET PAD!**

BEGINNER'S LUCK.

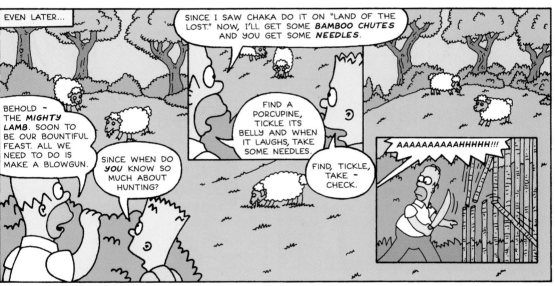

EVEN LATER...

SINCE I SAW CHAKA DO IT ON "LAND OF THE LOST." NOW, I'LL GET SOME **BAMBOO CHUTES** AND YOU GET SOME **NEEDLES**.

BEHOLD -- THE **MIGHTY LAMB**. SOON TO BE OUR BOUNTIFUL FEAST. ALL WE NEED TO DO IS MAKE A BLOWGUN.

SINCE WHEN DO **YOU** KNOW SO MUCH ABOUT HUNTING?

FIND A PORCUPINE, TICKLE ITS BELLY AND WHEN IT LAUGHS, TAKE SOME NEEDLES.

FIND, TICKLE, TAKE -- CHECK.

AAAAAAAAAAHHHHH!!!

HE DIDN'T THINK IT WAS FUNNY.

GOOD JOB, BOY! NOW WATCH AND LEARN. THE TRICK IS TO TAKE A DEEP BREATH.

PLUCK!

SHOONK!

AFTER ANOTHER UNSUCCESSFUL DAY...

OH, BOY. BANANA...*AGAIN*. WHAT ARE WE GOING TO DO TONIGHT, *KABOB* IT?

WHATEVER YOU DO, I'VE GOT DIBS ON THE PEEL.

HOMER, I HATE TO BE THE NEGATIVE ONE, BUT IT'S BEEN A *WEEK* NOW AND ALL WE'VE HAD TO EAT IS FIVE BANANAS AND A BUNCH OF STICKS.

HOW LONG CAN WE *SURVIVE* LIKE THIS?

SO WE'RE OFF TO A SLOW START. THESE BIOSPHERES TAKE A WHILE TO GET USED TO. YOU CAN'T EXPECT US TO LIVE HIGH OFF THE HOG IN THE *FIRST WEEK*.

QUE PASA, MI NEIGHBURRITOS! WE DECIDED TO GO MEXICAN TONIGHT. COME OVER AND GIVE THE OLD *PINATA* A WHACK.

TING TINGA-LING!

NO... AND THAT'S MEXICAN FOR *NO!*

HOMER, I THINK IT'S ABOUT TIME YOU LET NED *HELP* US. WE COULD WORK TOGETHER, SO WE CAN *ALL* ENJOY THIS EXPERIENCE.

YEAH, BECAUSE THIS SUCKS.

FLANDERS, I'M THE *KING* OF THIS FAMILY, AND IF THEY'RE GOING TO RELY ON ANYONE, IT'S GOING TO BE *ME!*

IF YOU CHANGE YOUR MIND, *MI* CASA ES *SU* CASA.

ZIP!

TOSS!

DON'T WORRY, WE'RE JUST *FINE*. WE'VE SURVIVED ONE WEEK; FIFTY-ONE MORE WON'T *KILL* US.

THAT NIGHT...

I'VE ALMOST GOT IT. I THINK I SEE SMOKE.

POP!

I *DID* IT! I SAID LET THERE BE FIRE, AND THERE WAS FIRE, AND IT WAS GOOD!

GEE, HOMEY, MAYBE I WAS A LITTLE TOO PREMATURE IN *DOUBTING* YOU.

POP!

SNAPPLE!

CROK!

WAY TO GO, DAD. THIS COULD BE A WHOLE NEW START FOR US.

ALL YOU *NAYSAYERS* DIDN'T BELIEVE IN ME. WELL, *THIS* WILL SHOW YOU...

WHOOOSH!

POP!

POP!

CRACK!

SIZZLE!!

SIZZLE!

LET'S JUST GO TO SLEEP.

THE NEXT MORNING...

ACTIVITY UPDATE!

PLOOP!

SNOW ANGEL **MAKING** ON OUR FRONT YARD IN TEN TICKLY TICKS OF THE CLOCK!

KRAK!

DAD, WHEN WE'RE DONE, CAN I SHOVEL THE YARD?

NO FAIR, LAST NIGHT HE GOT TO CLEAN THE DISHES.

STOP *QUARRELING*, CHILDREN. THERE ARE ENOUGH CHORES TO GO AROUND FOR EVERYONE!

MOM, I CAN'T SEE. MY EYELIDS ARE *FROZEN SHUT*.

SO ARE MY *NOSTRILS!* IF I SNEEZE MY *HEAD* WILL EXPLODE!

HOMER, THE KIDS ARE MISERABLE AND *I'M* MISERABLE. I THINK WE SHOULD GO TO THE FLANDERS'S AND LET THEM *HELP* US.

COME ON, MARGE, DON'T LET A LITTLE *FROSTBITE* AND *STARVATION* GET YOU DOWN. IF YOU LEAVE, YOU'LL JUST BE TELLING ME THAT I'M *NO GOOD*.

LATER, HOMER.

SORRY, DAD.

WHEN YOU SWALLOW YOUR PRIDE, YOU KNOW WHERE WE'LL BE.

LAZARUS RISING FROM THE GRAVE?

JESUS HEALING THE BLIND?

SOME GEEK WEARING A SHEET CARRYING TWO BOOKS?

YOU'RE ALL WRONG. IT'S *MOSES* BRINGING DOWN THE TABLETS FROM ON HIGH.

AWWWW...

DON'T FRET A SWEAT. WE STILL HAVEN'T HIT THE *NEW* TESTAMENT YET.

NEW TESTAMENT

AWWWW...

OH, NO! HE'S *BRAINWASHING* THEM! MAKE IT STOP!

I CAN'T. BUT YOU CAN. YOU HAVE TO SHOW YOUR FAMILY YOU'RE *RESPONSIBLE* AND YOU CAN TAKE CARE OF THEM.

BUT I'M A *LOUSY* DAD. EVERYTHING I DO JUST BLOWS UP IN MY FACE.

HOMER, FOLLOW ME. I'M GOING TO HELP YOU.

MAINTENANCE

I'M GIVING YOU *TWO* OPTIONS. BEHIND THAT WATERFALL IS A WAY OUT OF THE BIOSPHERE. YOU CAN LEAVE, GIVE UP ON YOUR FAMILY AND LIVE YOUR LIFE *RIDDEN WITH GUILT.* OR YOU CAN STAY HERE, GO BACK TO YOUR FAMILY AND SHOW THEM THAT YOU'RE THE *BEST* FATHER YOU CAN BE.

HOMER, YOU'RE ON YOUR OWN NOW. IF YOU NEED ANY MORE HELP, JUST LISTEN TO YOUR *HEART.*

POP

WELL, HEART, I'M GOING BACK TO SPRINGFIELD. MY FAMILY WILL BE BETTER OFF *WITHOUT* ME.

STUPID BIOSPHERE! THIS THING WAS SUPPOSED TO BE *EASY!* I'M JUST A LOSER...WITH A CAPITAL *LOO!*

MEANWHILE...

YOU KNOW, I'M REALLY STARTING TO *WORRY* ABOUT YOUR FATHER.

ARTS AND CRAFTS IN TEN MINUTES!

YEAH, AND THIS HAPPY ROUTINE IS GETTING OLD FAST.

IF I HEAR ONE MORE VERSE OF KUM-BA-YAH, I'M GOING TO BEAT SOMEONE WITH A *HYMNAL.*

THE FLANDERS HAVE BEEN NICE ENOUGH TO LET US INTO THEIR HOME. I THINK THE *LEAST* WE CAN DO IS PRETEND TO ENJOY OURSELVES.

BUT WHAT ABOUT *DAD?*

THIS *BITES!*

I DON'T KNOW, LISA. MAYBE YOUR FATHER JUST NEEDS SOME TIME *ALONE.* BUT FOR NOW, YOU KIDS PUT ON HAPPY FACES AND GRAB YOUR SMOCKS.

SPAK!

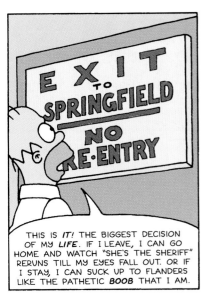

EXIT TO SPRINGFIELD
NO RE-ENTRY

THIS IS *IT!* THE BIGGEST DECISION OF MY *LIFE*. IF I LEAVE, I CAN GO HOME AND WATCH "SHE'S THE SHERIFF" RERUNS TILL MY EYES FALL OUT. OR IF I STAY, I CAN SUCK UP TO FLANDERS LIKE THE PATHETIC *BOOB* THAT I AM.

HEADS I WALK -- TAILS I STAY.

FLIP!

OKAY, TWO OUT OF THREE.

MEANWHILE, BACK AT THE CASA DE FLANDERS...

PUFF! PUFF!

SIZZLE! SIZZLE! CRACKLE-CRACK!

HEY, WHAT'S THAT *SMELL?*

JIMINY CHRISTMAS! THE HOUSE IS ABLAZE AND THE STAIRS ARE GONE! WE'RE *TRAPPED!*

NED, WHAT ARE WE GOING TO *DO?*

DIE!!!

OH, HOMER, I WAS SO *WORRIED* ABOUT YOU. I DIDN'T THINK YOU WERE GOING TO COME BACK.

I DIDN'T THINK SO EITHER, BUT I HAD A HEART TO HEART WITH MY HEART AND DECIDED THAT I'M NO LONGER GOING TO BE A FAT, LAZY, IRRESPONSIBLE FATHER. FROM NOW ON I'M GOING TO BE A FAT, LAZY, *RESPONSIBLE* FATHER!

WAY TO GO, HOMER!

DAD, YOU'RE THE BEST FATHER A KID COULD HAVE!

AND THE BEST HUBBY TOO!

WE'RE OUT! WE'RE SAVED! HOMER, YOU MUST BE *BLESSED.*

NAH, I JUST MADE A WISH UPON A *STAR*.

BIOSPHERE CANNED!

McCLURE SCANDAL

TEN WASN'T TOO MANY CLAIM **30** UNWED MOTHERS

THE END

BECAUSE YOU DEMANDED IT -- UNTOLD, UNTRUE STORIES FROM THE YEARS SEYMOUR SKINNER SPENT IN THE 'NAM, FIGHTING FOR THE AMERICAN WAY! IN THIS INSTALLMENT, SKINNER RECOUNTS A TALE OF MAN'S INHUMANITY TO MAN, PROPER JUNGLE HYGIENE, AND THE PIQUANT FLAVOR OF PROPERLY COOKED CHIPPED BEEF ON TOAST. ALL IS TOLD! NO PUNCHES PULLED! IN A TALE WE CALL...

SPARE THE ROD, SPOIL THE GRUNT!

THINGS ARE GOING TO *CHANGE* AROUND OUR BELOVED SPRINGFIELD ELEMENTARY. THE DAYS OF BIG SCHOOL GOVERNMENT ARE *OVER!* THERE WILL BE NO MORE *HANDOUTS!* THUS, I AM *ELIMINATING* THE HOT LUNCH PROGRAM. IF STUDENTS OF ECONOMIC NEED CARE TO DINE, THEY WILL BE ALLOTTED SEED FOR CROPS AND A TRACT OF LAND OVER BY THE SWING SET.

HOOLIGANS AND NE'ER-DO-WELLS WILL HAVE *NO PLACE* AT OUR SCHOOL! IN THAT SPIRIT, I WILL BE SPONSORING A THREE STRIKES AND YOU'RE OUT INITIATIVE FOR REPEAT SPITBALLERS, SWIRLY-GIVERS, AND THE LIKE! BUT, YOU MAY ASK, "WHAT OF EVERYDAY *DISCIPLINE* FOR THE OCCASIONAL CHATTERBOX OR CLOCKWATCHER, SKINNER? WHAT OF *POSITIVE REINFORCEMENT*, SKINNER?" WELL--

PADDLING OUR WAY TO A NEW AMERICA

SCRIPT
SCOTT M. GIMPLE

PENCILS
LUIS ESCOBAR

INKS
DAVID MOWRY

LETTERING
MIKE SAKAMOTO

COLOR
ELECTRIC CRAYON

MILITARY ADVISOR
MATT GROENING

-- *BEHOLD*, THE FUTURE OF DISCIPLINE IN SPRINGFIELD!

I'D LIKE TO PERSONALLY THANK CHIEF WIGGUM AND THE SPRINGFIELD POLICE DEPARTMENT FOR DONATING THIS FINE, STURDY PADDLE AS A PART OF THEIR "SPANKED STRAIGHT" ANTI-CRIME PROGRAM.

UMMM, PRINCIPAL SKINNER, I HAVE TO TELL YOU THAT THIS WHOLE BUSINESS OF PADDLING *WORRIES* ME. HITTING A CHILD -- FOR ANY REASON -- JUST SEEMS *WRONG*.

IF YOU WANT TO PUNISH UNRULY STUDENTS, HAVE THEM POUND ERASERS OR WRITE REALLY LONG ESSAYS ON TREES. WE'RE TRYING TO MOLD THEIR *MINDS*, NOT THEIR *BACK-SIDES*. BESIDES, IF CHILDREN ARE PADDLED FOR EVERY RULE THEY BREAK, BART WILL WIND UP WITH *PERMANENT PHYSICAL DAMAGE*.

PERMANENT *DAMAGE*, MRS. SIMPSON -- OR PERMANENT *CHARACTER*? DISCIPLINE IS RARELY FUN AND IT'S NEVER PRETTY. THE 'NAM TAUGHT ME THAT. LET ME TELL YOU A LITTLE STORY ABOUT DISCIPLINE. MAYBE THEN, YOU'LL SEE HOW IMPORTANT IT IS.

IT WAS *VIETNAM*, 1967! I WAS A FIRST-TOUR SERGEANT, LEADING A GROUP OF YOUNG GRUNTS THAT WEREN'T ALL THAT DIFFERENT FROM BART OR YOUNG MUNTZ!...

...THEY WERE **HOOLIGANS** THAT NEEDED TO TAKE A TURN FROM **OBLIVION** ONTO THE FREEWAY OF THE **STRAIGHT AND NARROW!**

NOW RINSE AND REPEAT, PRIVATE!

BY THEN I KNEW THAT WAR **STINKS,** BUT I MADE SURE THAT THE PRIVATES IN MY COMPANY **DIDN'T!** MY BOYS BATHED TWICE A DAY!

I TAUGHT MY BOYS TO **FIGHT!**

WE CONDUCTED **GROOMING DRILLS!**

I WILL NOT TOLERATE **BEGRIMED NAILS** IN THIS MAN'S ARMY!

TO KEEP THEIR MINDS SHARP, I ADMINISTERED THE OCCASIONAL **VOCABULARY TEST.**

NOW, WHO AMONGST YOU LUNKS CAN PROPERLY USE THE TERM **GENRE?**

UH, IT'S A DISTINCTIVE TYPE OR CATEGORY, ESPECIALLY OF LITERARY COMPOSITION.

IN THE END, PUNISHMENT WAS DISHED OUT AS REGULARLY AS RATIONS...

PLOP!

...MY CREDO WAS **SPARE THE ROD, SPOIL THE GRUNT!**

IT MADE THEM INTO **SOLDIERS!** ALAS, MY BOYS DIDN'T SEE IT THAT WAY...

SHINEX

A BAG OF CHIPS NOW

GRENADE DUTY? I HAVE TO SANITIZE THE LAND MINES TONIGHT!

OF ALL THE OUTFITS IN THIS ARMY, I HAD TO LAND IN SERGEANT SEYMOUR SPIC'N'SPAN SKINNER'S.

I'M SICK OF SHINING GRENADES.

I WAS MAILING A LETTER TO MOTHER WHEN I OVERHEARD THE BOYS TALKING.

HEE HEE! SNICKER! HAW HAW!

I TELL YA, FELLAS, THAT SKINNER IS A GRADE-A *EIGHTBALL*. THERE'S A *WAR* GOING ON AND HE'S BUSY MAKING US WAX OUR *KNEECAPS*!

THE ENEMY BETTER WATCH OUT! IF SKINNER CATCHES 'EM, HE MIGHT CUT THEIR HAIR!

HA HA HAW! HA HA HA HA HA HA!

CRUSHED, I RETURNED TO MY QUARTERS AND STEAM-CLEANED MY BOOTS. THE BOYS CONTINUED THEIR CHARCOALED REVELRY, WHEN ONE OF THE PRIVATES NOTICED SOMETHING IN THE NEARBY SHRUBBERY.

HEY, FELLAS, *LOOK!*

KRUSTY'S FAMOUS SAUCE

YUM IT'S BLUE!

CONDIMENTS FROM BACK HOME! *HOW?!*

I HAVEN'T SEEN A BOTTLE OF *KRUSTY'S FAMOUS* FOR *MONTHS!*

THERE'S MORE?

THERE'S MORE!

THE BOYS SCRAMBLED INTO THE JUNGLE FOR THE SAVORY SANDWICH DRESSINGS AND KETCHUPS, ROAMING FAR FROM CAMP IN THEIR MAD RUSH!

WHILE I MARTINIZED MY SOCKS, I HAD AN *EPIPHANY!* I DECIDED THAT I MUST TELL MY BOYS WHY *CLEANLINESS* WAS NEXT TO *GODLINESS!* WHY, A SOLDIER MUST BE BOTH A CRACK SHOT *AND* BANG-UP LATRINE DIGGER! BUT WHEN I RETURNED TO THE BARBECUE, I FOUND THEM...

GONE!

IT DIDN'T TAKE ME LONG TO FIGURE OUT WHAT HAD HAPPENED...

I HAD RECEIVED A MIMEOGRAPHED INTELLIGENCE REPORT ABOUT THE *CEYE-YUNG PRISONER CAMP* FORTY-FIVE CLICKS FROM THE BASE. I KNEW THAT IF THE BOYS HAD BEEN CAPTURED, THEY'D BE *THERE.*

I WAS RIGHT!

I SILENTLY CREPT INTO THE JUNGLE, USING MY COMB TO ERASE MY TRACKS, READY TO SPRING MY PLAN...

HEY, DO YOU SMELL SOMETHING?

I THINK IT'S...*OLD SPICE!*

YEAH... WHAT IS THAT?

LOOK!

RUSTLE!

RUSTLE!

SHIFT!

USING ITEMS FROM MY EXTENSIVE TOILETRY KIT, I CREATED A *WHOLE PLATOON!* THE NON-STAINING ANTIPERSPIRANT STICKS I SURROUNDED THE CAMP WITH GAVE THE ENEMY THE ODOR OF AN APPROACHING, OVERWHELMING FORCE!

THE TREES AND BUSHES I JERRY-RIGGED WITH MY NAIL CLIPPER, TOOTHBRUSH, DENTAL FLOSS, AND EAR WAX REMOVAL SYSTEM CREATED MY FAUX-PLATOON'S MARCH!

THOSE WHO TRIED TO RUN FELL INTO *LATRINE TRENCHES* I DUG AROUND THE CAMP!

SNIPERS LOOKING THROUGH THEIR SCOPES WERE BLINDED BY MY *ULTRA-SHINED HELMET!* I HAD TAKEN THE CAMP -- ON MY OWN -- USING THE SAME SKILLS I TRIED SO HARD TO IMBUE IN MY BOYS.

SOON, MY BOYS AND I TRANSFORMED THE P.O.W. COMPOUND INTO A *TRUE* DETENTION CAMP.

I will not practice Communist ideology
I will not practice Communist ideology
I will not practice Communist ideology
I will not pr

UH, SIR?

YES?

SIR, ON BEHALF OF THE BOYS, I'D LIKE TO THANK YOU FOR WHAT YOU DID. YOUR SPIC'N'SPAN SOLDIERING SAVED OUR SORRY BUTTS.

UH SIR, COULD I BORROW YOUR *COMB?* I WOULDN'T WANT TO APPEAR *SLOVENLY.*

GO AHEAD, SOLDIER, BORROW MY COMB. BE SURE TO USE THE *FIELD BARBICIDE* I BROUGHT IN MY PACK.

AS SEEN ON "SMARTLINE"

WHAT ARE YOU, NUTS OR SOMETHING?

Unwind your mind and leave your troubles behind at

Dr. Marvin Monroe's
E-Z ANALYSIS HUT

"Check your anxieties at the door and throw away the claim tag."

LOVED ONES' EATING HABITS DRIVING YOU GA-GA? BOSS'S LUNKHEADEDNESS MAKING YOU TENSE AND IRRITABLE? SELF-ESTEEM-O-METER ON EMPTY?

We <u>guarantee</u> you'll feel blissfully superior for at least 30 minutes, or your money back!

Try Dr. Monroe's special $79.95 workshops *du jour:*

MONDAY:
Guilt, Schmilt! Giving Your Superego the Old Head Fake

TUESDAY:
The Primal Scream: Keep That Racket Down, Willya?!

WEDNESDAY:
It's Not Your Fault: Shifting Blame the E-Z Way.

THURSDAY: Choosing the Right Preschool for Your Inner Child

FRIDAY:
Creative Denial: Hey, Forget It!

WEEKENDS: Dr. Monroe's Tough Love Retreat: Learn how to dish it out AND take it. (All family members must sign liability waiver.)

IN A HURRY?

When that panic attack just won't wait, tune up your neuroses for just $19.95 at the...

MONROE-TO-GO
JIFFY-KWIK 5-MINUTE DRIVE-THRU INTERACTIVE CENTERING AND FOCUSING WINDOW

Three caring and understanding lanes to choose from:
- Live Counselor (stuffed animal and kleenex optional)
- Video Counselor with remote control question-and-answer menu
- Speakerphone with counselor on audio cassette

(4-wheel drive vehicles add $5. Sorry, no big rigs or buses)

Looking for the perfect gift? Visit our

NOVELTY NOOK
Featuring officially licensed DR. MARVIN MONROE products...
"His" and "Hers" Foam Rubber Mallets • Rose-Colored Glasses • Easy-to-Assemble Isolation Tanks
AND FOR THE KIDS: Itchy and Scratchy's "My Very Own Nightmare" Journal

---

INSOMNIACS!
Try our 24-HOUR HOTLINE!
Soothing recorded counselors available around the clock!
1-900-QUIKFIX
95¢ per minute.
Touchtone phone required.

NUCLEAR POWER PLANT EMPLOYEES!

Don't miss Dr. Monroe's hit video cassette,
"Feeling Good About Your Radiation Level"
20% OFF
WITH THIS COUPON
(Valid weekdays only, 9 to 5. Must show proof of 10 years' minimum exposure. Blood sample may be required.)

Opening Soon! Dr. Monroe's
PSYCHO-PSNACK PSHOP!
Featuring...
• Prozac Shakes • Lithium Chip Cookies • Thorazine-On-A-Stick

---

YES! We have INTERACTIVE FAMILY ELECTROSHOCK THERAPY!

SMILIN' JOE FISSION'S Fun Corner

UP 'N' ATOM, BOYS 'N' GIRLS!

YOU KNOW HOW YOU HATE TO TAKE OUT THE GARBAGE NO MATTER HOW MUCH YOUR MOM NAGS YOU... WELL, HEH, HEH! WE GROWN-UPS ARE KINDA THE SAME WAY ABOUT GETTING RID OF OUR NUCLEAR WASTE!

CONSERVATION:
PIE-IN-THE-SKY TOMFOOLERY OR DANGEROUS EXTREMISM?

In fact, it's both! Conservation is both impractical (after all, who wants less power?) and economically risky. Remember, the more power you use, the more we make! That means jobs for many of our citizens—maybe even your parents—and toys, clothes, and allowances for children like you!

So relax and enjoy, and leave the power to us!

TODAY'S NUCLEAR BRAIN TEASER

Q: Where do you safely dispose of high-level liquid and solid radioactive waste?

A: If ANYONE has an answer to today's quiz, PLEASE contact the Nuclear Regulatory Commission as soon as possible!!!

HEY, KIDS! GRAB A PENCIL AND SEE IF YOU CAN SOLVE TODAY'S ATOMIC BRAIN TWISTER!

HERE IN SPRINGFIELD THE MANY BLESSINGS OF NUCLEAR POWER ARE AVAILABLE TO ALL, NO MATTER HOW LOWLY THEIR SOCIAL STATUS. BUT DO YOU KNOW WHO THE BIGGEST BENEFICIARY IS? CONNECT THE DOTS AND FIND OUT!

STORY
GARY GLASBERG

PENCILS
PHIL ORTIZ

INKS
TIM BAVINGTON

LETTERS
JEANNINE & CHRIS CROWELL UNGAR

COLORS
NATHAN KANE

BOY GENIUS
MATT GROENING

70

WHAT'S THIS ALL ABOUT?!

HE *STOLE* OUR *COMIC BOOK!*

GRABBED IT RIGHT OUTA MY HANDS!

I GOT CAUGHT UP IN THE HEAT OF *PASSION!* I THOUGHT I WAS IN *GYM CLASS!*

FOR HEAVEN'S SAKE, WILLIE, GIVE IT BACK! IT'S NOTHING BUT A STUPID COMIC BOOK!

DO YA REALIZE WHAT YER ASKIN', WOMAN? THIS IS THE LAST COPY OF *THE OYSTERIZER* ANYWHERE IN TOWN!

THE *WHAT?!*

THE OYSTERIZER, MA'AM. THE *GREATEST* UNDERGROUND COMIC TO HIT SPRINGFIELD ELEMENTARY IN *DECADES!!*

HEY!

AND WHO'S *RESPONSIBLE* FOR THIS PHOTOCOPIED *WASTE* OF *WOOD PULP?!*

THAT NIGHT...

D'OH! DARN *BATTERIES!* I COULD'VE SWORN I JUST CHANGED THESE LAST WEEK!

HURRY, HOMEY! SWITCH THE CHANNEL. OUR FAVORITE CONSUMER INVESTIGATOR IS ABOUT TO UNCOVER ANOTHER SPRINGFIELD BUSINESS SCAM!!

GOOD EVENING, FOLKS. I'M *DAVE SHUTTON.* ON TONIGHT'S *"EYE FOR AN EYE"* WE RAISE THE QUESTION "ARE THE ALUMINUM FOIL SWAN-SHAPED DOGGIE BAGS USED BY RITZY EATERIES A WASTE OF PRECIOUS RESOURCES?" STAY TUNED!!

MMM, DOGGIE BAGS!

AND WHERE DO YOU THINK *YOU'RE* GOING, BART?

OOPS!

UM...WELL... MILHOUSE AND I WERE PLANNING ON GOING TO THE BIG SPRINGFIELD *COMIC CONVENTION.* REMEMBER?

YOU'VE BEEN *SUSPENDED,* YOUNG MAN. YOU'RE NOT GOING ANYWHERE!

BUT YOU CAN'T *GROUND* ME! NOT *NOW!* THE COMIC CONVENTION IS THE MOST *IMPORTANT DAY* OF THE YEAR! IF WE DON'T PRESENT *THE OYSTERIZER* AT TONIGHT'S PORTFOLIO REVIEW, WE'RE *FINISHED!*

CRUNCH!

CRUNCH!

NOW, WHAT'S SO *GREAT* ABOUT A BUNCH OF MAKE-BELIEVE *SUPERHEROES,* ANYWAY?! YOUR *FATHER* IS THE BEST *HERO* A BOY COULD HAVE!

MMM, POPCORN GREASE!

BUURP!!

YOU BROKE *SCHOOL RULES,* BART SIMPSON! NOW GO TO YOUR *ROOM* AND DON'T COME OUT UNTIL THE CONVENTION'S OVER!

:SIGH: YES, MA'AM.

I GUESS SHE'S RIGHT. I MEAN, WHOEVER HEARD OF A GUY BECOMING A *MILLIONAIRE* BECAUSE HE CREATED A SILLY *CARTOON CHARACTER,* ANYWAY?!

LATER...

MAN, LOOK AT THE TIME! THE CONVENTION *CLOSES* IN TWO HOURS! WHAT AM I GONNA DO?!

YOUR *MA* DOESN'T KNOW NOTHIN', SQUIRT! THIS IS THE *CHANCE* OF A *LIFETIME!* BIG BUCKS! LIMOUSINES! *MILLIONS* OF KIDS *BEGGIN'* FOR YOUR *AUTOGRAPH!* YOU *GOTTA* BREAK OUTA THIS JOINT!!

POOF!

DON'T *LISTEN* TO HIM, BART! MOTHER KNOWS BEST! FAME AND FORTUNE QUICKLY CORRUPT! THERE'S MORE TO LIFE THAN VIDEO GAMES AND--

POOF!

GET *LOST,* HALO-HEAD! THE *DEVIL'S* RIGHT! THERE'S ONLY ONE THING LEFT TO DO!!

FLITZ!

BARTRON TO *MILBOT...BARTRON* TO *MILBOT!!* COME IN!

WHAT'S UP, BARTRON?

MEET ME AT THE *CONVENTION CENTER,* MILBOT. IT'S NOW OR NEVER!!

LATER...

SPRINGFIELD CONVENTION CENTER
COMICS EXPO

THIS IS IT, MAN. OUR *DESTINY* AWAITS!

CAN I GET A CONVENTION DOG FIRST?! I'M STARVED!

REGISTRATION AREA

GUESTS ↓   PROS ↓   GEEKS ↓

WHICH WINDOW IS FOR US?

WHOA!

GEEK

GEEK

I MUST BE *DREAMING!*

WELCOME TO THE COMICS EXPO!

AISLE 100

AISLE 100

AISLE 120

AISLE 120

HOW MUCH FOR THE MOTHMA-ZILLA, PAL?!

WHAT DO PEOPLE *DO* WITH ALL THIS STUFF??

THE SAME THING WE DO WITH OUR TOYS... BLOW 'EM UP OR PUT 'EM IN THE MICROWAVE!

SALE!

IN PERSON!
BURT LARUE
THE ORIGINAL RADIOACTIVE MAN STUNT DOUBLE FROM THE 1953 T.V. SHOW

YESSIR, THOSE WERE THE DAYS! THE SET WAS LIKE AN ORGY! WANNA SEE MY SCARS??

I HAVEN'T HAD TO SHAKE DIS MANY CLAMMY HANDS SINCE DA REPUBLICAN BARN RAISING AND LUAU IN '92!

GUEST

McBAIN THE ANIMATED SERIES

YOW! THAT *KORRELIAN PRIESTESS* CAN CLIMB INTO MY MOON FIGHTER ANYTIME!

LOOK, BART! MORE *FREE* STUFF!

GEEK

KRUSTY Comics

EXIT

ANY *BLOKE* THAT DOESN'T LIKE MY WORK CAN *CHOKE* ON HIS OWN VOMIT!

≈GULP≈

REMEMBER, IF THEY OFFER US A *CONTRACT*, STAY COOL! YOU DON'T WANT TO SEEM NERVOUS!

WHAT IF I THROW UP?!

BOFFO COMICS

PORTFOLIO REVIEW

I'M LENNY... THIS IS JOEL. TO YOU, WE'RE GODS. YOU'VE GOT *THIRTY-FIVE SECONDS* TO ENTERTAIN US. JOEL HASN'T SMILED IN EIGHTEEN YEARS. *GO!*

CLICK

LENNY HUFFS

JOEL BINX

CHECK IT OUT! WHEN MASTER SCUBA INSTRUCTOR *DIRK DAWSON'S* DEPTH GAUGE FAILS, HE LOSES CONSCIOUSNESS AND SINKS TO THE BOTTOM OF THE SEA.

PLUMMETING INTO THE DARKNESS, HE LANDS DANGEROUSLY CLOSE TO A SHIPWRECKED *NUCLEAR SUBMARINE* AND BECOMES TRAPPED INSIDE THE SHELL OF A NEARBY GIANT OYSTER!

MONTHS LATER, HAVING GONE THROUGH AN *ATOMICALLY* ENHANCED META-MORPHOSIS, THE OYSTER OPENS, GIVING BIRTH TO THE WORLD'S LAT-EST AND GREATEST MUTANT SUPERHERO... *THE OYSTERIZER!*

YOUR *STORYLINES* ARE SIMPLISTIC...YOUR *LAYOUT'S* POORLY CONCEIVED.

LENNY HUFFS

JOEL BINX

SO, WHAT ARE YOU TRYING TO SAY?!

WELL?

LENNY BOFFO COMICS

JOEL

I'VE SEEN MORE *INTERESTING* ARTWORK IN PUBLIC RESTROOMS!

LENNY HUFFS

PERHAPS I CAN INTEREST YOU TWO FEEBLE-MINDED *TODDLERS* IN SOMETHING OTHER THAN BRAIN PABULUM! THIS IS THE NEW *MASTERPIECE* FROM BOFFO! I CAN'T UNPACK THE PULITZER PRIZE WINNER FAST ENOUGH! HOW MANY CAN I PUT YOU DOWN FOR?!

THANKS, BUT I'VE AL-READY GOT ONE AT HOME!

WHAT ARE WE GOING TO DO, BART?!

FROZEN PEARL OYSTER SNACKS

WE'RE PAY-ING A VISIT TO *BOFFO COMICS,* MILHOUSE! ARNOLD LEACH *OWES* US BIG TIME!!

FROZEN

LATER...

BOFFO A DIVISION OF BURNS INDUSTRIES

UH-OH!! I THINK THE *GUARD'S* ON-TO US!

WOULD YOU LIKE FRIES WITH THAT BURGER, YOUNG LADY?!

NO PROBLEMO!

80

1 BILLION COPIES SOLD!

BART, I DON'T THINK ANYBODY'S GOING TO *BELIEVE* US.

ARE YOU KIDDING?! I BET LENNY AND JOEL CAN'T WAIT TO SAY THANKS!

CAN I HELP YOU?

TELL LEACH HIS *BOY GENIUSES* ARE HERE!!

I'M SORRY, BUT MR. LEACH IS ENTERTAINING GUESTS ON *THE PEARL* YACHT. IT'S A PARTY FOR THE COMIC'S CREATORS, LENNY AND JOEL.

THE COMIC'S CREATORS?! *AYE, CARUMBA!!*

THERE THEY ARE... *GET'EM!!*

WHOOOOA!

TELL LEACH HE'LL BE HEARING FROM MY *MOUTHPIECE!!*

LATER...

IT'S LIKE THIS, HUTZ. MILHOUSE AND I THOUGHT UP *THE PEARL*, DREW *THE PEARL*, AND SHOWED *THE PEARL* TO BOFFO A FEW MONTHS AGO! NOW THEY'RE *RICH* AND WE'RE NOT!

DARN CUBE!! IT'S BEEN *TEASING* MY BRAIN FOR TWENTY YEARS. MAKE IT STOP!!

WE *DEMAND* JUSTICE AND COMPENSATION! A LITTLE RECOGNITION! OUR PIECE OF THE MEGA-MOOLA PIE!!

HEY, WATCH THE OAK FORMICA!

THUD!

SPRINGFIELD GAZZETTE

PEARL SETS WALL STREET A-WHIRL

LET ME GET THIS STRAIGHT. YOU EXPECT ME TO *BELIEVE* THAT YOU TWO LITTLE *PIP-SQUEAKS* CREATED THE BIGGEST SUPERHERO IN THE HISTORY OF ENTERTAINMENT MERCHANDISING?!

YESSIR!

I *REFUSE* TO TURN THIS OFFICE INTO A DEN OF *LIE TELLIN'* GUYS AND *DECEIT-MONGERS!* NOW, *GET OUT!!*

PSSST! KID! MEET ME IN THE ALLEY. WE NEED TO TALK *BUSINESS*!

HUH?!

ALL RIGHT, WHAT'S THIS ALL ABOUT?!

THE DROID'S DUNGEON COMIC SHOP

½ OFF!

POST NO BILLS

THE PEAR

HIYA, BOYS! RE-MEMBER ME? I WORK FOR BOFFO COMICS.

YOU'RE *LENNY*! YOU *STOLE* OUR IDEA!

I KNOW I'M A BUM, BUT A CHARACTER LIKE *THE PEARL* DOESN'T COME ALONG VERY OFTEN!

YOU GUYS CREATED SOME-THIN' WORTH *MILLIONS* AND NOW *THE PEARL* NEEDS YOUR HELP!!

WHAT *KIND* OF HELP?!

YOU TWO COME TO **WORK** AT BOFFO AND SAVE **THE PEARL** FROM **FINANCIAL FAILURE!**

AND WHAT DO WE GET IN RETURN?!

CONTRACT
I, BART SIMPSON

CONTRACT
I, MILHOUSE VAN HOUTEN

MONTGOMERY BURNS OWNS BOFFO COMICS. YOU GUYS SAY NO, LEACH PULLS SOME STRINGS, AND BART'S OLD MAN IS **OUT OF A JOB!** UNDERSTOOD?!

THE PEARL

THAT'S **BLACKMAIL!**

THAT'S **BUSINESS!** TAKE IT OR LEAVE IT! WHAT'S IT GONNA BE?!

SIGN IT, DUDE. I'VE GOT AN IDEA!!

LATER...

YOU MEAN, THAT CRUMMY COMIC BOOK YOU USED TO WORK ON IS ACTUALLY **THE PEARL?!**

BART, THIS TIME EVEN I'M IMPRESSED!!

I KNOW IT'S HARD TO BELIEVE, SIS, BUT IT'S TRUE. BOFFO STOLE IT FROM RIGHT UNDER OUR NOSES!

NOW THEY'RE *BLACKMAILING* US INTO WORKING FOR THEM OR THEY'LL HAVE MR. BURNS *FIRE* DAD!!

THAT'S WHERE *YOU* COME IN, LISA!

SINCE YOU CAN'T GO *PUBLIC* YOURSELF, YOU HAVE NO CHOICE BUT TO PLANT A *SECRET MESSAGE* IN AN UPCOMING ISSUE ACCUSING LEACH OF *PLAGIARISM* AND *SLIMY BUSINESS PRACTICES!* BUT HOW?!

I HAVE AN IDEA!!

A FEW DAYS LATER...

GOOD MORNING, CONSUMER RESEARCHERS! ANYTHING *JUICY* IN TODAY'S MAILBAG?!

WEEKNITES CHANNEL 6 — EYE FOR AN EYE

WELL, MR. SHUTTON, I HAVE A COMPANY THAT CLAIMS ITS HIGH PRICED TOASTER WILL BURN THE IMAGE OF A RELIGIOUS LEADER INTO AN ENGLISH MUFFIN!!

NICE TRY, SON. BUT GIVE YOUR UNCLE DAVE SOMETHING HE CAN SINK HIS TEETH INTO!

MEANWHILE...

BART, WE HAVEN'T *SLEPT* IN DAYS! I CAN'T KEEP THIS UP MUCH LONGER!

HOLD ON, MILHOUSE! JUST A FEW MORE DRAWINGS!

THAT'S THE *SPIRIT*, SIMPSON! JUST A FEW MORE DRAWINGS. AND THEN A FEW *HUNDRED* MORE AFTER THAT!

BOSS

THANKS TO THAT *PARENTAL RELEASE* BURNS CONNED YOUR FATHER INTO SIGNING, *YOU'RE MINE!!*

SALES ARE RIGHT BACK ON TRACK, BUDDY!

WE COULDN'T HAVE DONE IT WITHOUT YOU, BART! IF YOU KNOW WHAT I MEAN?

KEEP UP THE GOOD WORK, VAN HOUTEN! IF YOU'RE NICE, I'LL PAY YOU IN BACK ISSUES!!

HA-HA!

COFF!

ARNOLD LEACH... DAVE SHUTTON, *EYE FOR AN EYE!* IS IT *TRUE* YOU *STOLE* THE IDEA FOR *THE PEARL?* WHO'S THE *RIGHTFUL HEIR* TO THE PEARL FORTUNE?!

CRASH!

WHO THE...?

WOO-HOO! GO GET HIM, DAVE!!

IT'S A LIE! I CAME UP WITH THE *CLAM GUY* MYSELF!

I WAS WOLFIN' DOWN SOME FISH STICKS WHEN IT CAME TO ME IN A DREAM! SO, SOME *KID* AT A CONVENTION HAD THE IDEA FIRST... PROVE IT!!

SHUT UP, YOU IDIOT!

WE DID IT, MILHOUSE!!

WEEKS LATER...

SIMPSON, I'M TEMPORARILY SENDING YOU TO WORK FOR MY *COMIC BOOK COMPANY*.

DON'T ASK ANY QUESTIONS! JUST DO AS YOUR TOLD BY YOUR NEW *SUPERVISOR!!*

MONTGOMERY BURNS

BUT, SIR...

GO!!!

WHY DO I HAVE TO GO WORK AT A DUMB COMIC BOOK FACTORY, ANYWAY?!

BOO

SIR, IT'S HOMER SIMPSON. MAY I COME IN?

SUITE 201

Boffo BOSS

MY BOSS IS PROBABLY SOME NASTY OLD STICK IN THE MUD!!

Boffo BOSS

BOY?!

HOMER!!

BART SIMPSON

THAT AFTERNOON...

MR. BURNS AND I STRUCK A *DEAL!* HE DOESN'T GET *PROSECUTED* AND I GET A COOL *SUMMER JOB* COMPLETE WITH A BALDING YET SOMEHOW LOVABLE ASSISTANT! PRETTY AWESOME, HUH?!

DONUTS

COL

BART, YOU'RE THE BEST SON...UM BOSS...A MAN COULD EVER HAVE!!

THAT'S *"MR. BART"* TO YOU!!

D'OH!

THE END

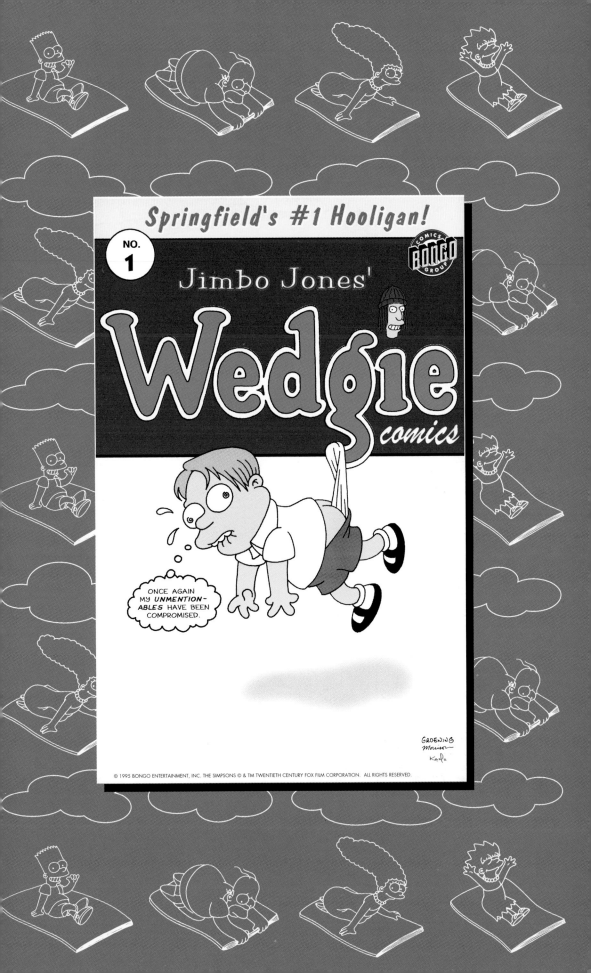

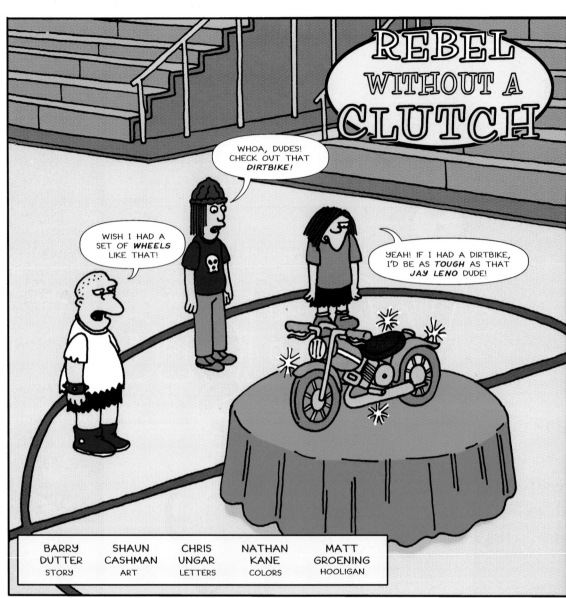

REBEL WITHOUT A CLUTCH

WHOA, DUDES! CHECK OUT THAT *DIRTBIKE!*

WISH I HAD A SET OF *WHEELS* LIKE THAT!

YEAH! IF I HAD A DIRTBIKE, I'D BE AS *TOUGH* AS THAT *JAY LENO* DUDE!

BARRY DUTTER	SHAUN CASHMAN	CHRIS UNGAR	NATHAN KANE	MATT GROENING
STORY	ART	LETTERS	COLORS	HOOLIGAN

YOU CAN FORGET THOSE *TAILPIPE DREAMS* OF YOURS, BOYS!

THIS DIRTBIKE IS THE *PRIZE* IN *SPRINGFIELD ELEMENTARY'S ANNUAL ART FESTIVAL & BAKE OFF!*

THE ONLY WAY YOU'LL BE RIDING *THIS* BABY IS IF YOU THREE *HOODLUMS* SUDDENLY LEARN HOW TO *EXPRESS* YOURSELVES *CREATIVELY!*

NOW, WHY DON'T YOU RUN ALONG! AND DON'T LET ME *CATCH* YOU GIVING ANY OF YOUR *INVOLUNTARY MUDBATHS!*

THOSE PUNKS ARE A *WASTE* OF TIME! THEY'LL NEVER *LEARN* ANYTHING!

SAY, THAT *REMINDS* ME -- EXACTLY WHY IS A *DIRTBIKE* BEING GIVEN AWAY AS A PRIZE IN AN *ARTS & CRAFTS SHOW*?

WE WANTED *ALL* THE KIDS TO ENTER, NOT JUST THE *ART NERDS!*

93

94

THE END!

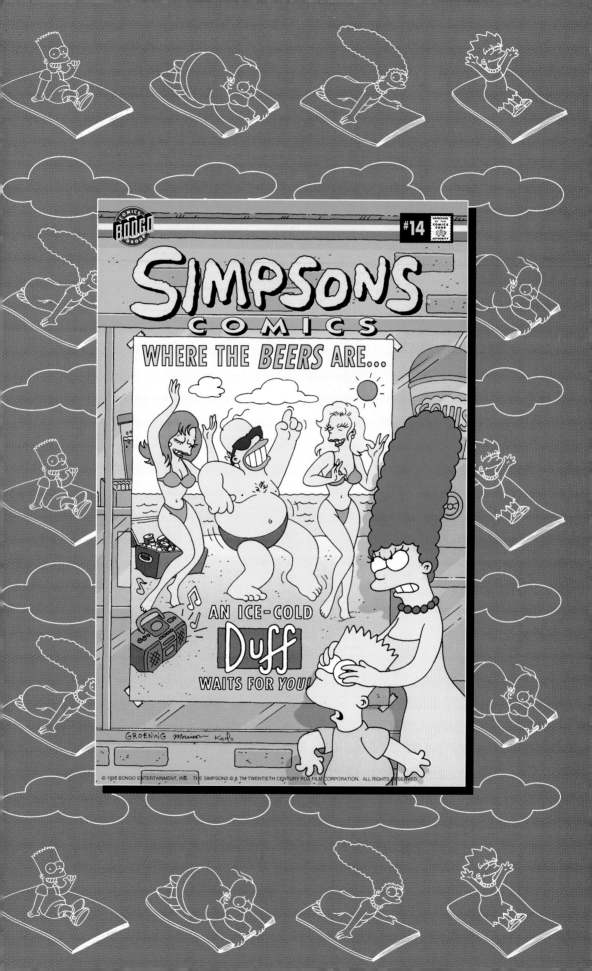

To Heir i$ Homer

SCRIPT	PENCILS	INKS	LETTERING	COLOR	MR. SALTY
JON AIBEL, GLENN BERGER & JEFF ROSENTHAL	CHRIS ROMAN	TIM HARKINS	JEANNINE CROWELL	NATHAN KANE	MATT GROENING

I'M NOT COMING TO DINNER.

AH, WHAT'S THE *MATTER?* YOU'RE ALWAYS *BEGGING* US FOR ATTENTION!

TRIXIE RUTHERFORD ASKED ME TO TAKE HER TO THE *SADIE HAWKINS DANCE*.

≡WHISPER WHISPER≡

I *KNOW* SHE'S DEAD! I STILL HAVE TO HONOR HER INVITATION. BESIDES, THERE'S A *MATLOCK IN MAYBERRY* SPECIAL ON AT NINE.

BUT WHAT'LL I TELL MARGE AND THE KIDS?

TELL 'EM I *DIED!*

I'M NO GOOD AT LYING. WHY DON'T *YOU* TELL THEM YOU DIED.

WAIT, THAT WON'T WORK...

...D'OH!

HEY! THANKS A *LOT* STUPID BRAIN!

SOON...

THAT SMELL...
IT'S...IT'S...MUSTARD
...AND PASTRAMI AND...

:SNIFF:

...MMMM...
DELI PICKLES.

C'MON,
NOSE LOCK
ON...

BINGO!

WHAT THE?...
THAT'S *MY* SAND-
WICH, CABBIE!

YAAAGH!

I...AM...
NOT...A...CAB
DRIVER!

D'OH!

HEY, MY
SUPPER! WHAT
AM I GOING TO
EAT FOR DINNER,
NOW?

HEY, HOW WOULD YOU LIKE
TO HAVE DINNER WITH MY
FAMILY? WE'RE HAVING
CASSEROLE.

WHAT
KIND OF
CASSEROLE?

UH, YOU KNOW, YUMMY, TASTY
CASSEROLE, MADE FROM...MMM...
CASSEROLE FOOD.

O.K.,
LET'S GO.

IN THE KITCHEN...

MARGE, WE'RE HOME. IS DINNER READY?

JUST ABOUT.

HOMEY, *THAT'S NOT GRAMPA!*

THIS IS *SAM.*

HOMER, THIS WAS SUPPOSED TO BE A *FAMILY* DINNER.

BUT, MARGE, THEY'RE BOTH *OLD!* WHAT'S THE *DIFFERENCE?*

≤MOAN≥

SOMETHING SURE SMELLS GOOD.

IT SURE ISN'T SAM.

THIS MUST BE HIS FIRST MEAL IN *WEEKS.* KIDS, WHAT YOUR FATHER DID WAS...UM...IMPULSIVE, BUT STILL VERY NOBLE.

YEAH, DAD SHOULD BE COMMENDED. HE HEARD THE DESPERATE PLEAS OF THE DISEN-FRANCHISED AND SAID...

SHOVEL! SNARF! SHOVEL!

MMM, GRISTLE!

AFTER DINNER...

IN **MY** FAMILY, WE USED TO SPEND EVENINGS CREATING OUR **OWN** ENTERTAINMENT. WE WOULD SHARE ALL OF OUR SPECIAL TALENTS AND ABILITIES BECAUSE WE HAD NO **TELEVISION**.

WE WOULD PERFORM MAGIC TRICKS...

WHAT'S THIS IN YOUR EAR, SON?

FLOOP!

COOL, MAN!

...SING SONGS, JUGGLE, YOU NAME IT!

LATER...

MARGE, THANK YOU FOR A LOVELY EVENING. IT TAKES A CERTAIN KIND OF COMPASSION AND DISREGARD FOR ONE'S PERSONAL SAFETY TO LET A TOTAL STRANGER INTO THEIR HOME.

I WILL NOT FORGET YOUR HUSBAND'S ACT OF KINDNESS.

GOOD-BYE, SAM.

BUT, SAM, WHERE WILL YOU **GO**?

DON'T WORRY ABOUT ME, I'LL BE JUST FINE.

WHOOOOSH!

WHOA, MAMA!

THE NEXT MORNING...

MR. SIMPSON! *MR. SIMPSON!*

SKRITCH SKRITCH

SLAM

MORNIN', HOMER. WANNA WATCH THAT MASTERFUL, RIB-TICKLING, SATIRIST KNOWN AS *KRUSTY THE KLOWN?*

≡MUMBLE≡

HEY! THEY'RE INTERRUPTING THE *CLOWNIEST CLOWN* ON EARTH FOR SOME LOUSY *GROWN-UP* STORY.

Special Report

BE *QUIET*, BART. *SPECIAL REPORTS* HERALD MONUMENTAL OCCASIONS IN ONE'S LIFE. IT COULD BE AN AN-NOUNCEMENT OF A PRECEDENT-SETTING CHANGE IN FOREIGN POLICY, THE DISCOVERY OF A CURE FOR A PREVIOUSLY INCURABLE DISEASE, OR...

WE INTERRUPT THIS PROGRAM, QUITE FRANKLY...

HEH, HEH

BECAUSE WE *CAN!*

...A FLAGRANT DISPLAY OF THE NEWS MEDIA'S TOTALITARIAN GRIP ON THE AIRWAVES.

OUR *TOP* STORY THIS MORNING CONCERNS *SAMUEL T. DUFF*, RECLUSIVE BILLIONAIRE FOUNDER OF THE *DUFF BEER EMPIRE*!

LOOK, IT'S *SAM*!

OH, MY *GOOD-NESS*!

WOW! WHO'D'A THOUGHT THAT HITCH-HIKING HOBO WOULD TURN OUT TO BE A BILLIONAIRE? *I* SURE DIDN'T SEE *THAT* ONE COMING!

ARE YOU SURE THAT'S HIM?

I *NEVER* FORGET A FACE!

HEY, IF THAT BUM WAS SO RICH, WHAT WAS HE DOING MOOCHING A FREE MEAL OFF OF *US*? LOUSY *CHEAPSKATE*!

HOMER, YOU SHOULD FEEL SORRY FOR HIM.

WHY SHOULD I FEEL SORRY FOR HIM, MARGE? HE'S A BILLIONAIRE.

A *DEAD* BILLIONAIRE.

SPRINGFIELD GAZETTE
DUFF KICKS CAN

MR. *DUFF*, A LIFETIME BACHELOR AND ALLEGED CAT-FANCIER HAS *NO* LIVING RELATIVES AND THEREFORE WAS THOUGHT TO BE *HEIRLESS*...

...*UH*, THAT IS... NOT *BALD*...JUST WITHOUT AN *HEIR* TO HIS *VAST FORTUNE*.

HOWEVER, WE HAVE LEARNED THAT THE BEER CZAR MADE A LAST MINUTE REVISION TO HIS WILL, LEAVING HIS *ENTIRE EMPIRE* TO ONE LUCKY SPRINGFIELD RESIDENT!

≥GASP≤

IT SEEMS THAT SPRINGFIELD'S *NEWEST* BILLIONAIRE IS AS RECLUSIVE AS HIS BENE-FACTOR. HE *REFUSES* TO BE INTERVIEWED AND SCURRIED BACK INSIDE WHEN FIRST ENCOUNTERING THE MEDIA MOB OUTSIDE HIS...MANSION.

HEH-HEH. ALLITERATION, A NEWSMAN'S POETRY.

RECORDED EARLIER

HOMER, DO YOU SEE WHAT *I* SEE?

YEAH, SO? IT'S JUST SOME NEWS GUY TALKING ABOUT SOMEBODY BEING PUT INTO THAT OLD GUY'S WILL, WHILE AT THE SAME TIME THEY'RE SHOWING A VIDEOTAPE OF *ME* GETTING THE MORNING PAPER.

IT'S NOT LIKE THEY SAID *I* INHERITED A WHOLE *BEER EMPIRE* AND *BILLIONS OF DOLLARS,* NOW IS IT, MRS. SMARTY-PANTS?

SO FAR, LITTLE IS KNOWN ABOUT THE NEW OWNER OF THE DUFF BREWERIES OTHER THAN HIS NAME, *HOMER J. SIMPSON!*

D'OH!

I'M SORRY ABOUT THE SMARTY-PANTS THING, MARGE. I WAS WRONG.

I'M A *BILLIONAAAAIRE!* I'M A *BILLIONAAAAIRE!* I'M A *BILLIONAAAAIRE!*

WELL, WHAM-BAM, THANK YOU, *SAM!*

MEANWHILE...

SMITHERS!

HERE IT IS, SIR. YOUR OTHER CONTACT LENS.

AHH! ONCE AGAIN IN THE LAND OF DEPTH PERCEPTION!

LOOK AT THIS CHICANERY, SMITHERS. A WORKING STIFF TAKES IN A HAPLESS HOBO, GIVES HIM A QUAINT, SUBURBAN SUPPER AND THE NEXT DAY HE'S BEQUEATHED A BILLION DOLLAR BEER FORTUNE.

ONLY IN AMERICA, SIR.

HMMM, MAKES YOU WONDER IF THAT'S WHAT THE FOUNDING FATHERS *REALLY* HAD IN MIND WHEN THEY CAME UP WITH THAT WHOLE "*FREEDOM*" CONCEPT.

WHO IS THIS *HOMER SIMPSON*?

HE'S ONE OF OUR SAFETY INSPECTORS.

WELL, HE'S *FIRED!* NOW LET'S SEE HIM TRY TO LIVE ON A MEASLY *BILLION DOLLARS!*

SO, THIS DO-GOODER THINKS HE CAN RUN A BREWERY. WELL, AS MUCH AS I ENJOY WATCHING MONEY AND POWER CORRUPT A MAN'S SOUL, I'LL *NEVER* BE ONE-UPPED BY SOME *HOMER-COME-LATELY!*

SMITHERS, I HAVE A PLAN.

THE NEXT DAY...

DUFF BEER

"CAN'T GET ENOUGH OF THAT WONDERFUL DUFF"

SPRINGFIELD PLANT

IS EVERYONE READY FOR THE V.I.P. TOUR?

YEAH, YEAH, YEAH! DO I GET FREE BEER?

WOO HOO!

HA, HA. OF COURSE YOU DO, MR. SIMPSON. AFTER ALL, IT'S YOUR BREWERY NOW.

BART, WHY DO I HAVE A VISION OF BEING ON A TALK SHOW DESCRIBING THIS VERY MOMENT AS THE LOW POINT OF MY CHILDHOOD?

C'MON, LISA. DEEP DOWN YOU CAN SMELL A MONEY MAKING-OPPORTUNITY AS WELL AS I CAN.

:MOAN:

BEHIND THIS FOUNTAIN LIES THE SOURCE OF OUR BEER'S DISTINCTIVE TASTE--THE CRYSTAL CLEAR WATERS OF DUFF SPRINGS!

SINCE 1973, WHEN SKYROCKETING COSTS FORCED US OFF THE MUNICIPAL WATER SUPPLY, DUFF BEER HAS COME TO YOU STRAIGHT FROM NATURE.

NO TRESPASS PROPERTY OF Duff ENTERPRISES

NO SWIMMING, WADI FISHING OR--WATE!

CLOSED BY ORDER OF PRES. TRUMAN

QUARANTINED

LATER...

HERE'S WHERE DUFF BEER IS PROPERLY AGED TO ACHIEVE ITS FINE, SMOOTH CHARACTER. TAKE A TASTE, MR. SIMPSON.

MMM... *CHARACTER!*

WHOA, THERE, MR. SIMPSON! WE'D BETTER LEAVE SOME FOR OUR *PAYING* CUSTOMERS.

HUH? OH, YEAH. HEE-HEE.

ANY QUESTIONS, MR. SIMPSON?

LET'S SEE... I CAN WORK WHENEVER I WANT, DRINK A LOT OF FREE BEER, UM...

WHEN DO WE MEET THE *NORWEGIAN G-STRING GIRLS?*

A SIX-PACK OF SHAME.

MR. SIMPSON, THOSE GALS AREN'T *REALLY* FROM NORWAY. THEY'RE JUST THREE SCANTILY CLAD WOMEN FROM OUR MARKETING DEPARTMENT. BUT, THEY SURE DO SELL THE DUFF!

THIS IS IT, MR. SIMPSON, THE MOMENT YOU HAVE BEEN WAITING FOR.

CHUGFEST?

NO. THE *BOARD OF DIRECTORS* IS READY TO SEE YOU.

MR. BURNS! WHAT ARE *YOU* DOING HERE?

SURPRISE, SIMPSON. MEET THE PROUD OWNER OF *FORTY-NINE PERCENT* OF DUFF INDUSTRIES.

WHO?

ME, YOU IDIOT!

OH. WAIT A MINUTE... LET'S SEE, FORTY-NINE PERCENT... OUT OF ONE HUNDRED PERCENT... CARRY THE ONE...

MARGE, IF HE OWNS FORTY-NINE PER...

YOU OWN *FIFTY-ONE* PERCENT.

D'OH!

I *KNEW* IT WAS TOO GOOD TO BE TRUE.

WAP!

DAD, *YOU* OWN MORE.

WOO HOO!

I OWN *MORE*! I OWN *MORE*!

I WOULDN'T BREAK OUT THE CHAM-PALE JUST YET.

YOU MAY BE SAM'S CHOSEN HEIR, BUT AS EXECUTOR OF THE WILL AND THE ONLY DUFF OFFICER ALIVE AND UN-SCATHED BY THE *SYRINGE-IN-THE-BOTTLE* INCIDENT, I MUST DECIDE IF YOU ARE *TRULY WORTHY* OF HIS FORTUNE.

NO FAIR! YOU *KNOW* ME!

YES. I KNOW YOU AND I'VE DEVISED SOME SIMPLE, YET PRACTICALLY *INSURMOUNTABLE* TESTS FOR YOU.

TESTS?

SOON...

NOW, MR. SIMPSON, ALL YOU HAVE TO DO IS TAKE A LITTLE NAP.

A NAP, HUH? *NOBODY* NAPS LIKE *HOMER*!

YES, OFF TO *DREAMLAND*, SIMPSON.

A BRILLIANT IDEA, SIR. HE'LL NEVER FEEL THAT BEER NUT UNDERNEATH ALL THOSE CUSHIONS.

CAN'T...GET... COMFY...

FIDGET!

STRUGGLE!

SPROING!

AAAGH! LOOK OUT!

MMM... *BEER NUT*!

UNBELIEVABLE! HE PASSED THE TEST!

DAMN HIM AND HIS *SEN-SITIVE BUTT*!

BONK!

A FEW TESTS LATER...

NOW, FOR YOUR FINAL CHALLENGE, A SIMPLE *TASTE TEST.*

CORRECTLY IDENTIFY THE DIFFERENT TYPES OF DUFF BEER FROM THE SELECTION WITHIN, AND THE FORTUNE IS YOURS!

TODAY, I CONSIDER MYSELF *THE LUCKIEST MAN ON EARTH!*

DUFF RED!

DUFF ICE!

DUFF... SSSPECIAL RESSSERVE!

HERE YOU GO, MR. SIMPSON, JUST ONE LAST BREW AND YOU WILL *HAVE* YOUR BLASTED EMPIRE.

A QUARTER DUFF DRAFT, AN EIGHTH DUFF DRY...AN EIGHTH DUFF MALT...AN EIGHTH DUFF LAGER...AN EIGHTH DUFF CHRISTMAS ALE...AND...AN EIGHTH, NO A QUARTER...DUFF AMBER FIRE-BREWED BARLEY EXPORT, WHICH IS ONLY SOLD...IN *CANADA!*

I'M AFRAID HE'S RIGHT, SIR.

BLAST HIS TASTE BUDS! I *MEAN* IT, SMITHERS. I WANT YOU TO FIND SOMEONE TO *BLAST* HIS *TASTEBUDS!*

THE NEXT MORNING...

HEY, DAD, GET OVER YOUR HANGOVER AND LOOK AT THESE REPORTS I FOUND IN SAM'S FILES.

I DON'T HAVE A HANGOVER, LISA, THIS IS THE WAY ALL EXECUTIVES WORK.

WELL, IF YOU CAN FIND TIME IN YOUR BUSY SCHEDULE, I THOUGHT YOU MIGHT FIND IT INTERESTING TO SEE RECENT REPORTS FROM THE BOARD OF DIRECTORS.

OOOH, ROBOTS!

ROBOT DESIGN

VETO

I must reject the Board's recommendation for an automated plant in favor of maintaining a bountiful job base for the people of Springfield.

Signed,

Samuel Duff

LOOK! THERE'S A LETTER FROM SAM!

MEANWHILE...

Duff   Duff

I'M NOT KIDDING YOU BOYS, MY OLD MAN CAN EAT TWO-DOZEN JELLY DONUTS IN ONE SITTING.

YOUR FATHER REALLY MUST HAVE A WORKING MAN'S DIGESTIVE TRACT.

SO, YOU FELLAS GOT ANY SUGGESTIONS FOR THE NEW MANAGEMENT TEAM?

BART, JUST KEEP EVERYTHING THE WAY MR. DUFF LEFT IT. I WOULDN'T CHANGE A THING.

SMITHERS, QUICKLY, WE MUST *DO* SOMETHING. SIMPSON IS DRIVING MY BREWERY INTO THE *GROUND!* WE'VE NO TIME TO LOSE.

WHERE DO YOU WANT THESE?

ROBOTS

PROPERTY OF SALON DES PRESIDENTS EURO KRUSTY LAND

ROBOTS

WE DIDN'T ORDER ANY *ROBOTS!*

OH, YES WE DID. *I* ORDERED THEM. I REVIEWED THE BOARD'S PLAN FOR AN AUTOMATED BREWERY AND OVERTURNED SAM'S VETO. HEH, HEH, US ROCK'N'FELLA TYPES GOT TO STICK TOGETHER, EH, BURNSY?

SMITHERS, I WILL NOT HAVE MY BREWERY OPERATED BY THAT LARD-BOTTOMED...

HEY!

~TAFT~
HE NEVER VETOED DESSERT

HE WAS TALKING ABOUT *TAFT.*

OH.

I WAS NEARLY *TARRED AND FEATHERED* FOR THINKING UP THAT AUTOMATION SCHEME. IF HE IMPLEMENTS IT, HE WILL BE THE MOST *REVILED* MAN IN SPRINGFIELD.

THOUGH IT PAINS ME TO *LOSE* THAT DISTINCTION, I AM HATCHING YET *ANOTHER* PLAN TO TAKE MY RIGHTFUL PLACE AS DUFF CHAIRMAN.

SMITHERS, HOW DO YOU FEEL ABOUT GOING *UNDERCOVER?*

I THOUGHT YOU'D NEVER ASK, SIR.

AH, *SIMPSON*. I WANT TO HAVE A LITTLE EXCHANGE OF IDEAS... *YOUR* IDEAS WILL BE EXCHANGED BY *MINE*.

B-B-BUT... I STILL RUN THIS COMPANY. REMEMBER, *FIFTY-ONE* PERCENT.

YAAAGH!

WHAT GOOD IS CONTROL OF A FACTORY FULL OF DISENCHANTED *BOOZEHOUNDS*? TAKE A GOOD LOOK, SIMPSON. YOU'RE REIGN OF *ERROR* IS OVER.

NO ONE WILL BUY YOUR PRODUCTS, NO ONE WILL WORK IN YOUR FACTORY, AND YOUR PRES-IDENTIAL *FRIENDS* WILL BE DESTROYED.

DOWN WITH HOMBR J. SMPLETON NU 24 DUNKIN'

UNFAIR TO IRON EX-PRESS

BUT IT'S STILL *MY* BREWERY.

SNAP

GOOD, GOOD! I'M GLAD TO SEE THERE'S STILL ENOUGH FIGHT IN YOU TO MAKE THIS AMUSING. GIVE IN SIMPSON! SELL ME YOUR SHARES AND MY TAKEOVER OF THE DUFF EMPIRE WILL BE *COMPLETE*!

AND IF I SAY *NO*?

AH, I SEE SAM HAS TAUGHT YOU *WELL*.

IT'S POINTLESS TO RESIST, SIMPSON. YOU *MUST* GIVE IN.

ALL SHARES

THE NEXT DAY...

THREE HUNDRED DOLLARS IS A LOT OF MONEY, HOMEY. WE CAN *STILL* CARPET THE BASEMENT.

IT'S NOT THE MONEY, MARGE. IT'S THAT I *FAILED*... *AGAIN!* AND AT SOMETHING AS SIMPLE AS RUNNING A BILLION DOLLAR BEER EMPIRE.

IT WASN'T A TOTAL LOSS, DAD. I LEARNED THAT MINDLESS AUTOMATONS WILL NOT MAKE HUMAN LABORERS OBSOLETE.

YEAH, AND I GOT TO EXPERIENCE THE LIFE OF A NE'ER-DO-WELL PLAYBOY SPONGING OFF THE FAMILY FORTUNE.

AND I GOT TO SEE THAT I LOVE MY HUSBAND, NO MATTER *WHERE* HE WORKS...OR DOESN'T. MAYBE MR. BURNS WILL GIVE YOU YOUR OLD JOB BACK.

NO WAY. HE MUST THINK I'M THE BIGGEST DOPE IN THE WORLD.

HELP WANTED

Springfield Gazette

DUFF NOT DEAD

CLAIMS 'JUST SLEEPING'

ELSEWHERE...

HOW CAN THIS BE? HE *DIED* OVER A *WEEK* AGO!

A RARE OCCURRENCE, SIR. I'M AS SURPRISED AS YOU ARE.

THIS MEANS THAT SIMPSON NEVER *LEGALLY* CONTROLLED DUFF! AND TO THINK, I GAVE HIM *THREE-HUNDRED DOLLARS*! THAT MAN IS SMARTER THAN HE LOOKS, SMITHERS. FIND OUT IF HE WOULD ACCEPT A POSITION AT THE NUCLEAR PLANT.

YOU *COULD* EMPLOY THE ROBOTS, SIR.

I RUN A *NUCLEAR POWER PLANT*, SMITHERS. I CAN'T LEAVE THE SAFETY OF MILLIONS IN THE HANDS OF *UNTHINKING MACHINES*! THIS TOWN DESERVES NO LESS THAN...WHAT WAS HIS NAME AGAIN?

SOON AFTER...

WELCOME BACK HOMER!

ZZZZZZZ...

THE END

GRAMPA SIMPSON
AND HIS CRANKY PAL JASPER IN

Nostalgia ain't what it used to be

SCOTT SHAW!	TIM BAVINGTON	CHRIS UNGAR	NATHAN KANE	MATT GROENING
STORY & PENCILS	INKS	LETTERS	COLORS	PACKRAT

126

THAT *TEARS* IT! I'VE NEVER *SEEN* SUCH A CON-GLOMERATION OF WORTHLESS *FOOLISHNESS, CLAPTRAP AND FOLDEROL* IN ALL MY BORN DAYS!

YOU MEMORY-MONGERS ARE BLEEDIN' PEOPLE *DRY* IN THE NAME OF *NOSTALGIC FUN! FIE* ON YOU! *FIE,* I SAY!

KRUSTY MANIA EVERYTHING FOR THE DISCERNING CLOWNOPHILE

OWHH...MY CHEST HURTS...

ATTABOY, OLD-TIMER...JUST KEEP *RANTING...*

YOU'RE NOT GIVIN' *ABE* SIMPSON THE BUM'S RUSH *THAT* EASY! I'M CALLIN' *LARRY KING!*

TOSS

HEY! DON'T FORGET, WE'RE FEEBLE!

SO MUCH FOR *THAT* OLD PEST!

YEAH, BUT WAS HE *RIGHT? HAVE* WE BECOME A GREEDY, MERCENARY LOT, WILLING TO SELL THE VERY *ESSENCE OF CHILDHOOD* TO TURN A PROFIT? COULD WE *CHANGE* OURSELVES, MAKING *ALTRUISM* OUR COMMON GOAL?

SLAM.

NAHHHH!!!

LATER, AT *THE ANDROID'S DUNGEON* COMIC BOOK SHOP...

BACK ISSUE SALE

HEY KIDS!

HEY, KID. YOU'RE *BART SIMPSON* AREN'TCHA?

WHO THE HELL WANTS TO KNOW?

NO CHANGE FOR NEXT DOOR LAUNDROMAT

RADIOACTIVE MAN

CHECK OUT THE LATEST ISSUE OF *NOSTALGIA FANATICS WEEKLY* -- ISN'T THAT YOUR *GRANDFATHER?*

NOST... WEEKLY NATIO

LAST MONTH SPRINGFIELD'S COLLECTORAMA SHOW WAS DIS-RUPTED BY A GERIATRIC PSYCHO-LOGICAL TERRORIST. THE UNIDEN-TIFIED TROUBLEMAKER'S ANTI-SOCIAL BEHAVIOR SENT THE THRONG INTO A DEEP STATE OF EMOTIONAL DES-PAIR. EVEN THE MOST HARDCORE COL-LECTOR WAS TOO DISCOURAGED TO PURCHASE A SINGLE ITEM! THIS MAY BE THE WARNING SIGNAL OF AN IMMIN-ENT MARKET CRASH THROUGHOUT THE WORLD OF INVESTMENT-LEVEL COLLEC-TIBLES! ALL MEMORABILIA DEALERS AND COLLECTORS ARE URGED TO KEEP A LOOK-OUT FOR THIS SWORN ENEMY OF OUR LIVELIHOOD AND PASSION.

ARTIST'S DEPICTION OF TERRORIST.

COOL, MAN! I ALWAYS KNEW GRAMPA HAD IT IN 'IM!

BACK AT THE SPRINGFIELD RETIREMENT CASTLE, (SECOND FLOOR, THIRD ROOM ON THE LEFT)...

I STILL CAN'T GET OVER ALL THOSE *GULLIBLE ANAL RETENTIVES* FORKING OVER THEIR *LIFE SAVINGS* TO *SUPPLEMENT* THEIR RIDICULOUS *COLLECTIONS OF GEEGAWS* AND *THINGAMABOBBERS!*

DUPS

TERIYAKI

BUT COLLECTING *BEEF JERKIES OF THE WORLD*...NOW, *THAT'S* A HOBBY!

THE END